'Vivake has tried appreciably to budge the human conscience. The book is not only worth reading but also worth collecting.'

—Sudhanshuji Maharaj
Founder, Vishwa Jagriti Mission (World Awareness Mission)

'Vivake Pathak's book is an interesting read...I am sure many would find it enriching.'

Sagarika Ghose
—Senior Editor, CNN-IBN

'Unlike other books that claim to reveal God, *God and Destiny* shows God, not the way to God; it does not speculate but prove what God is; and it gives not many but one, not imaginary but real, definition of God. ...This book will also be a delight for people who are not sure about the meaning of destiny and those who believe in destiny but don't have enough logic for their belief.'

—Sabhajit Mishra
Active member of the Indian Council of Philosophical Research and the author of The Anguished Freedom

'Stephen Hawking once said that he believes in a God that is embodiment of the laws of the universe. Now *God and Destiny* has precisely and comprehensively revealed the God in which Hawking and many other scientists and philosophers have believed. ...Vivake has revived the exact definition of the uncertainty principle and revealed how it has been misinterpreted and misused through all these years. He has made it clear that "uncertainty principle" is a misnomer and the principle is no threat to determinism. Never before I was more convinced that the universe is completely deterministic. ...Delivering the knowledge of God and destiny, this is one of the most enlightening books ever written.'

—R.A. Singh
Former professor of physics, vice chancellor of Awadh University, and chairman of UP Higher Education Service Commission

'Whatever happens in the universe, including in our lives, is not only governed but preordained by God and is inevitable—this is the pinnacle of knowledge. ...this is the knowledge that gives birth to complete devotion in God, frees people from shackles of ego or vainglory, and leads them to peace and salvation; and this is the knowledge that *God and Destiny* has delivered finally.'

—Hariharkripalu Tripathi
Brahmarshi *(a title for a saint of the highest order);*
Mahamahopadhyaya *(a title for the teacher of the teachers);*
Acharya; Trustee, Kashi Vishwanath Temple Trust, Varanasi

GOD AND DESTINY

THE SUPREME KNOWLEDGE

God has been discovered
Your future is predestined and unchangeable

VIVAKE PATHAK

Rupa • Co

Published 2009 by
Rupa . Co
7/16, Ansari Road, Daryaganj,
New Delhi 110 002

Sales Centres:
Allahabad Bangalooru Chandigarh Chennai
Hyderabad Jaipur Kathmandu
Kolkata Mumbai Pune

Typeset in 1Stone Serif 10 pts. by
Mindways Design
1410 Chiranjiv Tower,
43 Nehru Place
New Delhi 110 019

Printed in India by
Rekha Printers Pvt. Ltd.
A-102/1 Okhla Industrial Area, Phase-II
New Delhi-110 020

To my parents,
Dr Karuna Shanker Pathak and Mrs Urmila Pathak,
and my brother, Dr Vikas Pathak,
who have helped me more than they could

CONTENTS

PREFACE

THE CONCEPT OF GOD AFFECTS EVERY HUMAN BEING IN SOME WAY OR the other, to some extent or other. People believe in him and have faith in him; fear, adore, pray, and worship him; think, speak, and write about him; and undertake holy and horrible missions in his name. Yet they do not know who or what he actually is. Billions of people want to and need to know God. To fulfil this need is the primary aim of this book.

God and Destiny is the first book that tells correctly and exactly what God is and reveals his true attributes and influence. In the process it also shows that whatever has to happen in the universe in the future, including whatever has to happen in anyone's life in the future, is predestined by him and is unchangeable. After the revelation of God, it takes people through an analysis of some nuclear beliefs of major theistic religions of the world to let them see the truth in as well as behind these beliefs.

General public is the primary audience of the book. It is meant for all irrespective of their educational level, religion and nationality. The topics covered in the book belong broadly to the fields of philosophy, religion, and physics and specifically to metaphysics, determinism, philosophy of religion, philosophical theology, philosophy of physics, and quantum mechanics. People related to the above fields form the secondary audiences of the book.

God and Destiny takes people to God through steps; it is based on sound, unbiased, undistorted facts, logic, and reason; and it is intended to be simple, fluent, clear, sharp, and conclusive. The style adopted is me-to-you, the reader being addressed in second person.

Part A of the appendices contains scientific proof, discussions, and findings related to the predestinedness and prediction of the future. And Part B of the appendices contains a brief detail of how I realised the absolute predestinedness of the future and how I found God.

The knowledge of God and destiny is the supreme knowledge not only because God is the supreme being but also because it is the knowledge of the state of everyone's being. It not only sets people free from the blind faith about God and destiny, but showing them that whatever happens in the universe is predestined by God and is unchangeable, it sets a foundation in them for freedom from anxiety, worry, tension, fear, and so on and illumines their way to unwavering, everlasting lively peace. Thus, it is the apex of all knowledge—the supreme knowledge.

VIVAKE PATHAK

Part 1
Introduction

1

THE AGE OF IGNORANCE IS OVER

It happened slowly and steadily:
walls that I felt disappeared;
boundaries that I knew dissolved;
holy light filled the dark.
He guided me to a different world,
situated beyond the edge of time,
abode of unwavering lively peace,
land of never-setting sun divine.
Give me your hand;
let me take you there.

THOUSANDS OF YEARS HAVE GONE SINCE GOD WAS FIRST IMAGINED. SINCE then the concept of God has been influencing unbelievably large portions of thoughts and activities of humanity. Your mind is full of innumerable stories, notions, and beliefs about him developed through human history, but he himself has remained a mystery for you. Countless people have tried to find him out but all in vain. The time of such ignorance is over. God is not interested in hiding anymore: now I shall let you know him and his true attributes and influence.

In the night of ignorance, some people have been thinking of themselves as closer or dearer to God on the basis of their religion, faith, community, character, and so on. God, whom I shall take you to, is not the God of people of any particular religion, faith, or school of thought. He is not a heritage of only humankind either. He is one and the same for everyone. He is the God of every human being, every living being, every living and nonliving being—he is the God of every being. You will know him irrespective of your caste, creed, community, religion, gender, social status, economic status, occupation, nature, character, and behaviour.

Alas! You have been deceived so much in God's name. He was not known to anyone, yet many people claimed knowing him or realising him; being in contact with him; being his messenger, relative, or representative; or even being his incarnation or embodiment. Since they were ignorant of God, they could not point towards him; so they told people that being a supernatural power, he is generally beyond perception and only those who have paranormal power, sixth sense, or pious soul can realise him. They devised innumerable weird, difficult, impracticable, and thorny paths for people to prepare them by making their souls holy to realise him.

Enough of your deceiving others or being deceived by others in his name! God is not beyond normal perception. He exists and is perceivable to everyone. Prayer, virtuous deed, desirelessness, austerity, penance, and so on are of no use in knowing him. You need not have any paranormal power, sixth sense, or holy soul to realise him. To lead you to the knowledge of the supreme being, neither have I devised any difficult, thorny, or slippery path for you, nor shall I ask you to undergo any type of austerity or penance. To know him, what you have to do is just to listen to what I say with an attentive and open mind.

In the beginning, to let you get a general concept of what the world has believed to be God, I shall present before you short summaries of what eight major theistic religions of the world say about him and the set of the most important epithets added to him by the majority of theists of the world, because he is God not of any particular religion but of all the religions.

I shall show you that God had never been known to anyone and all that had been said, written, and believed about him is hypothetical. To open you up, to decrease your blind faith, to increase your receptivity, and to prepare you further to know him, I shall answer the questions that this raises, such as if he was not known to anyone, why and how did people ever start to imagine his existence? what were the reasons of any person's claim of knowing him, having a link with him, or being his incarnation? how did our holy books that are seen as containing his orders, words, or will by many come into existence? and how were the epithets that are commonly believed to be describing him ('almighty', 'creator', 'eternal', 'omnipresent', 'omniscient', 'all-good', and so on) added to him?

As I said before, God is not beyond normal perception. He exists in reality and is perceivable to everyone. To take you to him, I shall involve you in a process of search or identification, but I shall not leave you midway with a future promise. Not only shall I let you know him exactly and precisely, but I shall also explain with the help of a number of examples why any other being cannot be God.

In the history of humankind, hardly anything might have been thought, discussed, said, and written about more than God might have. Since he was not known to anyone, people belonging to different religions and residing in different parts of the world added not completely but to notable extents different sets of epithets to him and developed different beliefs, concepts, and stories about him. After I let you know him, I shall take you through an analysis of the key portions of all that has been said, written, and believed about him to let you identify the truth in it.

Since God himself was unknown, the epithets added to him formed the nuclear portion of whatever was believed about him in general. What highlights their importance is that the small unanimity found among people of different faiths is confined mostly to his epithets—the only thing that shows that people all over the world have believed in one and the same God—but in absence of this knowledge, you could have never been sure whether any of his particular epithets was true to him or not. After letting you know him, the first thing I shall do is to show you which of some most significant epithets added to him by the theists, such as 'almighty', 'creator', 'eternal', 'omnipresent', 'omniscient', and 'all-good', describe him correctly and which are absurd to be added to him, and thus I shall reveal the attributes that are truly possessed by him.

Mostly whatever has been said, written, and believed about God lies within the domain of religion. In the age of ignorance, people have been having fierce but inconclusive debates and conflicts on who knows more about him, whose religion is better and deeper, and whose religion is closer to him. I shall let you know not only him and his attributes but also how correct or incorrect the basic concepts of each of the major theistic religions—Christianity, Confucianism, Hinduism, Islam, Judaism, Sikhism, Taoism, and Zoroastrianism—about God are. It will also give you an opportunity to compare the correctness of what your religion says about him with what other religions say about him.

There happen to be some beliefs that lie at the core of any religion because they play a vital role in its propagation and sustenance and also because they differentiate it from other religions. For example, many followers believe about certain person or persons, especially for the propagator or propagators of their religion, that they were close to or in contact with God; were his messenger, relative, or representative; or even were his embodiment or incarnation and about their key religious books that they contain his orders, words, or will. While analysing the correctness of important religious beliefs, I shall let you see how logical or absurd these two beliefs are.

Around the central religious beliefs lie the beliefs about the paths and ways of realising God. I shall show you the reasons of the propagation of some of such beliefs as about prayer, desirelessness, and virtuous deeds and their vainness for his realisation.

The concept of God provides living sap to theistic religions. Lastly, I shall discuss briefly the worth that will be left with these religions after I let you know God, his attributes, the truth behind the claims some persons made about knowing him or being his representative or incarnation, and the futility of the paths and ways proposed by them for realising him.

The main purpose of this book is to let everyone know God. To solve this purpose, the topic 'destiny' is also dealt within it to a significant extent.

The concept of destiny, if not as old as, is not much younger than the concept of God. Through human history, different people have believed in destiny to different extents, most people have had a keen desire to know their future, and countless people have been involved in the business of prediction of the future, even if it was not proved that the future is predestined. For the revelation of God, in this book, I shall show that the future is predestined and unchangeable, and thus I shall try to bring destiny out of the ambit of belief and disbelief.

You know that your future is affected by the decisions you make at present, and you think that since you have the capability to change your decisions, you yourself have the authority to change your future too, to the extent it depends on your decisions. No, it may disappoint you but it is not true. Before I present a universal proof of the predestinedness of the future, I shall let you see how destiny comes true in your life through your own will. It is true that it is you who makes the decisions, but it is also true that while doing so you act just like a tool. I shall show you that the decision you make in any particular situation is predestined and unchangeable and so is the future that results from that decision. The authority you think you possess to change your decisions is purely illusory, and so is the capability you feel you possess to change your future. You just cannot change your decisions or your future from what is predestined.

By mentioning that I shall present a universal proof of the predestinedness of the future, I mean I shall prove that whatever has to happen in the universe in the future, whether it is related to living things or nonliving things, including phenomena such as thoughts, ideas, plans, and feelings, is predestined and unchangeable or inevitable. Yes, I shall show you that your future is as unchangeable as your past is—that is, you, anyone, or anything cannot change the number, magnitude, or intensity of successes and failures; achievements and losses; joys and sorrows; and even dreams, thoughts, ideas, and plans of your future life from what is predestined.

I shall proceed to take you through a discussion on the possibility of prediction of the future, and finally at the end of the part related to destiny, I shall introduce you to the potential that the knowledge that the future is predestined and unchangeable possesses to affect the way of your thought and life.

The relation between God and destiny has always been a matter of great discussion. People have been wondering that if God is almighty, what role destiny might have to play in the course of events, and vice versa, that is, if everything is predestined, where does the almighty God fits in. This confusion will end now, as I shall show that it is the almighty, omnipotent, or supreme God who not only governs whatever happens but is the master of destiny of all the living and nonliving things that exist.

In the appendices, I shall present a scientific proof of the predestinedness of the future, show the vainness of the objections that can be raised against the proof on the basis of the principle of indeterminacy, and reveal what poses the ultimate limit to the accuracy with which the future can be predicted. In the process I shall explain the real meaning of the principle of indeterminacy in reference to the corporeal world and unravel how physicists have been misinterpreting and misusing it since its finding.

The task this book has to accomplish is not only to deliver the knowledge about God and destiny, to remove blind faith about them, and to end the conflict and violence going on in the world in his name but to lead everyone to deep and lasting inner mental peace—how much reason will you be left for tension, worry, anger, and so on if you know that whatever happens in the universe, including in your life, is predetermined by God and is inevitable?

Along with the proof of the theorem that the future is predestined and unchangeable, Part 2 contains discussions on other topics related to destiny. Revelation of God and other related topics have been dealt with in Part 3. As I have pointed before, both topics 'proof of the predestinedness of the future' and 'revelation of God', seemingly entirely independent, are actually deeply interrelated—former being one of the foundation stones for the latter. Therefore, for your thorough understanding of the topic 'revelation of God', which has been dealt with in Part 3, you are advised to go through Part 2 first.

Part 2

The Future is Predestined and Unchangeable

2

THE REACH OF DESTINY

No dream is seen,
no path traversed,
no tear does fall,
no smile blossoms
beyond the script.

LET THE STATEMENT 'THE FUTURE IS PREDESTINED AND UNCHANGEABLE' be termed the *theorem of destiny*.

When I make the statement of the theorem of destiny, 'The future is predestined and unchangeable', I use 'future' as universally applicable, which comprises every phenomenon, event, or happening that has to occur in the complete future of the whole universe. 'Future' does not adopt any double standard in including the future of an animal, a plant, a mountain, a planet, a star, or any other thing in its ambit along with your future. Besides, it stands for the complete future, without excluding any timespan or even a single instant.

In reference to you, 'future' means every detail of your future life, including your future successes, failures, relations, and accidents—even including your future thoughts, ideas, feelings, and imagination.

The term 'predestined' in the statement signifies that the future is predetermined or that it is determined or decided beforehand, not yesterday or the day before yesterday but infinite time before the present.

It is very important to understand the meaning of 'unchangeable' in the statement. It means that not only whatever has to occur is predestined but not even a single bit of change can be introduced in its programme by anyone or by any means. In this respect, the future is similar to the past. As you cannot change whatever happened in the past, you cannot change whatever has to occur in the future from what is predestined. Factors, such as, your hard work, perseverance, discipline, intelligence, and planning, with which you think that you make, determine, or decide your future, are themselves predestined and inevitable tools to bring about your predestined and inevitable future. Therefore, you, anyone, or anything cannot change the number, amount, and intensity of successes and failures, achievements and losses, joys and sorrows of your future life from what is predestined.

Thus, in detail I can state the theorem of destiny as

> Whatever has to happen in the universe in the future, whether it is related to living things or nonliving things, including abstract phenomena, such as thoughts, ideas, plans, and feelings, is predestined and unchangeable.

I shall prove this (the theorem of destiny) thoroughly in Chapters 4 and 5. A discussion on prediction of the future is on hand in Chapter 6. In the last chapter of this part, Chapter 7, I have discussed how the knowledge that the future is predestined and unchangeable will affect the way of your thought and life. But before all that, in the next chapter, Chapter 3, I shall show you how destiny comes true in your life, leaving you optionless in terms of the decisions you make, the works you do, and therefore the results you achieve.

3

YOU CANNOT CHANGE YOUR FUTURE

My destiny plays with me in such a way
I feel I play with my destiny.

BASED ON THE EXTENTS OF THEIR BELIEF IN DESTINY, PEOPLE CAN BE divided into three groups. The first group is of those who believe in destiny, even if they do not have a solid logical ground to do so. The third group is of those who disbelieve in it. Most people stand between the above two extremes—they constitute the second group.

People of the first group think that everything happens according to destiny. On the contrary, a person belonging to the third group says, 'Life is not guided by destiny. Of course, there are few happenings that affect our life but that are not in our control, such as natural calamities, economic and social status of our parents, our mental ability, and accidents and diseases, but these are matters of chance and have nothing to do with destiny. For the time being, if you keep them aside, you will find that in most cases and to large extent, a person decides the course of her life herself and makes her destiny according to her desire with the help of her planning, hard work, perseverance, and discipline. She herself is responsible for her successes and failures. The future is neither predetermined nor unchangeable. A person determines her future according to her desire. She changes it with the help of her hard work and will if she wishes to do so.'

Whether you believe in destiny or not, you will agree that your future is determined by the following:

- factors that are not in your control, such as natural calamities, economic and social status of your parents, your mental ability, and accidents and diseases
- whatever you do at present, whether you call it work, hard work, perseverance, or by any other name

You can ask, 'How can my future be predestined if it gets affected by the events that are not in our control and that occur randomly or just by chance? How can my future be predestined and unchangeable if it is determined by the works that I perform at present based on the decisions that are in my control and that are changeable? Can't I change my future by changing my decisions about what I have to do?'

In the next chapter, I shall show you that the future is predestined and the factors that determine it, whether you have control on them or not, are very predetermined and inevitable. Before that, in this chapter I shall show that your works and actions and your decisions behind them, about which you think that they are in your full control, are predetermined and inevitable and so is the future to the extent it depends on them. Therefore, for the time being, let us keep aside the factors that affect your future but are seemingly not in your control.

YOU AFFECT YOUR FUTURE THROUGH YOUR DECISIONS

You do not do anything just at random. Except for your reflex actions, first you make a decision of what and how to do and then you try to perform according to your decision. The process of first deciding and then doing goes on continuously.

Many a time, when you have time, you are conscious of the decision-making process, and if the decision you have to make is important, you spare time to think consciously to decide. In your daily busy life, when you do not have enough time to sit and think, the decision-making process goes on automatically, even if you do not consciously take part in it.

As you know, your future gets affected by whatever you do at present. Since you work according to your decisions, it is basically your decisions with the help of which you affect your future. You may think that since the power and right to decide as well as to change your decisions is vested in you, it is you who makes, decides, or changes your future at your own will. You are wrong if you think so. The freedom that you think you enjoy in decision making is illusory. The decision you make in a particular situation is predetermined and invariable, and so is the future to the extent it depends on your decision. An analysis of the decision-making process will make this clear.

THE DECISION-MAKING PROCESS IS LIKE A TUG-OF-WAR

At most steps of your life, you have multiple options before you about what you have to do. In any such situation, from the group of options before you, you select that one for action about which you think that it will prove to be the most appropriate. Here I have used 'most appropriate' instead of 'best' because many a time the decision-making process is a compromise, when you have to sacrifice the best option in favour of the most appropriate one.

The factors that take part in the decision-making process are elements of your personality as well as that of the situation that you undergo. Most of them are listed as follows:

1. your
    - desires
    - fears
    - likes
    - dislikes
    - capabilities
    - weaknesses
    - knowledge
    - experience
    - qualifications
    - farsightedness
2. the feelings you have for others
3. the total time available for making the decision

Under various degrees of influences of your desires, fears, likes, dislikes, feelings, and so on; keeping in view your capabilities, weaknesses, and qualities; assisted by your experience and knowledge; and using your farsightedness, you calculate the most appropriate option.

At every instant during the decision-making period, one or another option occupies the status of the most appropriate one. The analysis or the decision-making process goes on until one of the options decisively succeeds in occupying this status or until its further propagation becomes impossible due to urgency of action. In any case, the option that occupies the status of the most appropriate one at the end of the decision-making period is adopted for action. Thus, at any instant during the decision-making period, including at its end, the option acquiring the status of the most appropriate one is determined by mainly the following factors:

1. your
   - desires
   - fears
   - likes
   - dislikes
   - feelings for others
2. the assessment you make of your capabilities and weaknesses
3. the assistance your knowledge, experience, and qualifications provide you with
4. the analysing power of your brain in terms of your farsightedness
5. the time that has elapsed since you started the effort to come to the decision

On the whole, the decision-making process is like a tug-of-war among your desires, fears, likes, dislikes, feelings, and so on acting as forces. Your farsightedness, your experience, your knowledge, the importance you give to your qualifications, and the assessment you make of your capabilities and weaknesses take the side of one or other of these forces during this tug-of-war. At any instant during this tug-of-war, the option towards which the resultant of these forces point acquires the status of the most appropriate one. At different instants during this tug-of-war or during the decision-making period, since these factors and the degrees of their influences on you are likely to be different, their resultant may point towards different options as the most appropriate one. The option that is finally pointed at as the most appropriate option at the end of the decision-making period is adopted for action.

THE DECISION YOU MAKE IS PREDESTINED AND UNCHANGEABLE

The resultant of a definite set of forces is predetermined and unchangeable. To give a simple example, if you put a four-kilogram weight on one scale and a five-kilogram weight on the other scale of a particular traditional balance, the resultant is predetermined and unchangeable—invariably, the five-kilogram weight will lift the other one to a predetermined height from itself, and the pointer on the middle of the beam will point at a predetermined angle from the vertical direction. So the option pointed at as the most appropriate one by the resultant of a definite set of factors that take part in the decision-making process, which have definite degrees of influences and which get involved in a tug-of-war as forces, too is predetermined as well as unchangeable. At a definite instant during the decision-making period, including that at its end, since all these factors, with their own degrees of influences, taken together form a definite set, the option towards which their resultant points as the most appropriate one is predetermined as well as unchangeable. Thus, being pointed at by the resultant of the definite set of factors that take part in the decision-making process—which have definite degrees of influences, which act like forces, and which get involved in a tug-of-war-like tussle—the option that acquires the status of the most appropriate one at the end of the decision-making period, which is adopted for action, is predetermined and unchangeable. Since the factors that take part in the decision-making process or that determine your decision are elements of your personality and the situation that you face, it can be said that when you with a definite personality undergo a definite situation with a definite set of options, the option with which you come out as most appropriate for action is predetermined and inevitable or unchangeable.

I have red, blue, and yellow cards before me:
all my future depends on my choice.
I think for hours, days, and weeks,
and at last I put my finger on
one that is already chosen for me.

YOU CANNOT CHANGE YOUR FUTURE

When you are put in any particular situation, you try to work or perform actions according to the decisions you make; besides, as I showed in the previous section, when you with a definite personality face a definite situation, the decision with which you come out as the most appropriate one for action is itself predetermined and unchangeable; so when you with a definite personality undergo a definite situation, the work or action that you perform is also predetermined and unchangeable.

Your works affect your future, and since you try to work according to the decisions you make, it is basically your decisions with which you affect your future. Since the decisions you make and the works you perform according to them at present are themselves predestined and unchangeable, your future to the extent it depends on them is predestined and unchangeable.

You have most probably been living with the illusion that it is you who holds the right to change your decisions, course of your actions, and therefore your future; but as I showed, you have no authority to change your decisions and the course of actions you perform according to them, so you cannot at all change your future too from what is predestined.

Your present tells the story of the decisions you made in the past. Try to recall your past decisions. On the touchstone of time, many of them proved to be good, and some of them boomeranged, proving to be disastrous. Recall a decision that led to ugly results and that today makes you think that instead of it if you had selected any other option, your life would have been quite different, of course quite better. There is no place for such ifs and buts in life. Today, not only can you not change that decision, but also if you look back and place yourself back in that time, with the same personality (knowledge, experience, farsightedness, and so on) that you had, in the same situation that you had faced, and with the same options that you had before you, then you will find that the option you had selected was lighted, shone, or crying out to be the most appropriate, that is, inevitable or unchangeable. The following example will make it clear to you:

Example 3.1

Y is a chartered accountant. She has developed a successful, growing accounting and consulting company of her own. The only offspring of Y is X, who is fifteen years old. He is good at studies and equally good at lawn tennis, in which he has won a few prestigious junior-level championships.

The time has come for X to decide whether he has to take tennis as his full-time career, leaving studies aside, or he has to continue studies, keeping tennis just as a hobby. He is passionately interested in tennis, and he is keen to take it up as a career. His mother knows that nothing is certain in taking a sport as a career and that he is so good at studies that he will be able to become a chartered accountant and, owing to his capabilities, he will be able to take care of her well-established business. She is also an ideologue. She has an ideology that parents should not force their decisions on their children, mostly because she herself had led her life in accordance with her wishes and ambitions and had been successful. Therefore, neither forced by his mother nor heeding to her advice, under the influence of his extreme interest and confidence in tennis, X selected it as his career.

He underwent extensive training and started to take part in senior-level tournaments. He tried hard for twelve long years but could not win even a single prestigious tournament, although he was very good at the junior level. His career as a tennis player was a failure.

Then, when he was twenty-seven, he decided to quit tennis and join his mother's business, where he had to start from scratch. When he was beginning to learn something, his mother died of a massive heart attack. An important assistant of hers took it as an opportunity and launched a company of his own, taking away many of the professionals as well as business contacts of her company. Since X lacked the professional knowledge and experience needed to revitalise the company in this time of crisis, it collapsed. The money obtained by auctioning it was enough just to return the loans his mother had taken for its expansions.

Ultimately, a boy who dreamt of being a tennis superstar ended up being a tennis coach for kids, losing also his mother's well-established business. All this was mainly because of the decision he had made when he was fifteen. Now he does not tire repenting and shedding tears for that decision, thinking that had he selected the other option, studies, he would have been leading quite a better life, managing and expanding his mother's business.

All this sorrow, even if it is natural, is improper because not only can X not change that decision today but also the decision was not at random. There were distinct and solid reasons behind it. It was a logical conclusion of a decisive tug-of-war among the following factors:

1. immense interest of X in tennis
2. his capabilities shown by his achievements at junior-level tennis
3. his confidence that he would be able to achieve excellent future in the field he was about to enter
4. the ideology of his mother that parents should not force their decisions on their children
5. keeping her business in her mind, her suggestion to her son that continuing his studies and entering the field she herself was in would be best for his future

The first four were in favour of the decision, and the last one, against it. Since every factor that could affect the decision actively took part in the decision-making process and the resultant decisively and invariably pointed towards the option he selected, there is no reason X would have come out with the other option as the most appropriate one. In other words, the option selected by him as the most appropriate one was predetermined and invariable, and so was his future to the extent it was affected by that decision.

RE-EMPHASISING THE UNCHANGEABILITY OF YOUR FUTURE

You saw that when you with a definite personality undergo a definite situation with a definite set of options, your decision, the option with which you come out as the most appropriate one for action, is predetermined and unchangeable and so are the works or actions you perform and the future to the extent they depend on that decision. It means that immaterial of the number of times you with the same personality undergo the same situation with the same set of options before you, each time you come out with the same decision, that is, the same option as the most appropriate one for action, performing the same work or action, which leads to the same future consequences.

Most of the factors that take part in the decision-making process change with time—some change automatically, such as your desires, fears, likes, dislikes, and experience, and others change as a result of your efforts, such as your knowledge and qualifications. It is only because of these changes in you caused with the passage of time that if you encounter the same situation with the same options at different times, each time you may come out with a different option as the most appropriate one. In other words, if the set of all the factors that are a part of your personality and that take part in a decision-making process is not allowed to change with time, irrespective of the number of times you encounter a particular situation with the same options before you, each time you will come out with the same option as the most appropriate one for action.

In your life if you come across the same situation with the same options to choose from for the second time, you may come out with a different option as the most appropriate one this time because even if the situation and the options are same, you are not same as before. Now you are equipped with the knowledge and experience of the result yielded by your previous decision. If actually no change has taken place in you in terms of the factors that take part in the decision-making process during this period or if the changes that have come in you during this period are erased, you will undoubtedly once again come out with the same decision as the most appropriate one. This can rarely be demonstrated because on one hand it is hardly possible that no change occurs in you in a definite timespan in terms of the factors that take part in the decision-making process and on the other hand it is practically impossible to erase such changes. Nevertheless, if any such thing occurs, it automatically proves that the decision with which you come out in a particular situation is predetermined and invariable and so is the future to the extent it depends on that decision. If you try to recall, you may trace a few such examples of your own life. The following is one from mine:

Example 3.2

I was playing chess on a computer. After a few initial moves, I found that I was in a very strong, almost winning, position. But only three moves after that, the contest became double-edged. Keeping in mind the twin objectives of maintaining my advantage as well as defending my position from the opponent's threat, after carefully thinking for some time, I made a move. Let me term this move as *D move* (decisive move). Computer's reply to this move was quite foolish. As a result, I won the game in the next few moves.

Not more than a week after that, I was playing chess against the same computer program. Once again the same game was repeated. I realised this when I had to make the crucial D move. Once again the contest was double-edged. I remembered that I had won that game, but I could not remember the next move or the D move. It was the turning point. I knew that if I could remember the D move, I could easily win the game. I tried hard to recall but all in vain. Seeing that door closed, once again I carefully and deeply analysed the situation and made a move. As soon as the computer replied, it flashed into my memory that the move that I had made was none other than the D move and that the computer had replied with the same foolishness as it had done in the previously played game. Thus, in the next four moves, I again won the game.

It was an occurrence of rare possibility that the first few moves of this game were exchanged in the same way as they were done in the previously played game because a chess program is designed to reply each time in a different way in a similar situation until a few initial moves have been exchanged. After that its reply in a particular situation is mostly the same, according to the sequence of logic mentioned in it, of course, when the game is played with a particular level.

On the other hand, even if I could not remember it, I once again made the D move in the same situation in the second game because the factors taking part in the decision-making process, that is, my intelligence, experience, and so on, had not changed to any considerable extent in this period of one week. In fact, not only the D move but all the moves I made in this game (including the first few moves, in which the program could have presented a variation) were respectively identical to those of the previously played game.

Once again it is endorsed that at any particular stage of life in any particular situation, the option that is intelligible to you as the most appropriate one to be adopted for action is predetermined and invariable and your future, to the extent it depends on it, is predetermined and unchangeable.

• • •

Other than your deeds performed according to your decisions, factors that determine your future are those about which you think that they occur randomly or just by chance, and therefore you think that the future to the extent it depends on them too will occur by chance. Contrary to your belief, not even a single event in the whole universe occurs at random; or every past, present, and future event of the universe is predetermined as well as inevitable. Now I shall show you how.

4

NOTHING WILL EVER HAPPEN BEYOND DESTINY 1

Tomorrow if
the sun will wake in the east and sleep in the west,
the shy moon will again peep through my window,
people will sow for each other thorns and flowers,
spring will return with new tender buds,
some stars will die and new ones will be born,
explosions and fireworks will amuse the space,
unknown will give birth to unexpected,
nothing will come up with a lot of nothing,
how can anything else happen tomorrow?

IN THE LAST CHAPTER, YOU SAW HOW THE DECISIONS THAT YOU MAKE, the works or actions that you perform according to your decisions, and your future to the extent it depends on them are predestined and unchangeable. In fact, as I have stated before, including in the form of the theorem of destiny in Chapter 2,

The future is predestined and unchangeable. ... (4.1)

which is also stated in detail as

> Whatever has to happen in the universe in the future, whether it is related to living things or nonliving things, including abstract phenomena, such as thoughts, ideas, plans, and feelings, is predestined and unchangeable. ... (4.2)

Basically, this {the theorem of destiny [(4.1) or (4.2)]} is what I shall show you in 'Nothing Will Ever Happen Beyond Destiny'.

I have proved the theorem of destiny in two ways, putting them in this chapter (Chapter 4) and the next one (Chapter 5), under the headings 'Nothing Will Ever Happen Beyond Destiny 1' and 'Nothing Will Ever Happen Beyond Destiny 2' respectively, the latter being a bit more advanced than the former, yet, to be understood, none of them needs any type of specialisation.

This chapter is independent and complete in itself, whereas the next one uses the basic assumptions and concepts and the examples presented here. Thus, I would suggest that to understand thoroughly and get a feel of how the future is predestined, go through this chapter first.

OBJECTIVE

In this chapter while proving the theorem of destiny [(4.1) or (4.2)], I shall prove that

1. (a) Not only that
        i. The future is predestined and unchangeable.
        but also
        ii. Whatever happened in the universe in the past was predestined and unchangeable.
        and
        iii. Whatever is happening in the universe at present is predestined and unchangeable.
    or
    (b) Whatever happens in the universe, whether it is related to living things or nonliving things, including abstract phenomena, such as thoughts, ideas, plans, and feelings, is predestined and inevitable or unchangeable.
2. To change what has to occur in the future is as impossible as it is to influence the universe by something that is not a part of it.
3. Immaterial of the number of times the universe acquires or be imparted the same identity that it had at any instant in the past, each time from that instant, it will exhibit the same phenomena, events, or happenings as it exhibited in the past from that instant onwards.

IDENTITY

Generally, it is better to use a short term for a phrase that has to be used repeatedly. In addition, to maintain the smoothness of readability, it is recommended to use, for the repeatedly used phrase, a term whose actual meaning resembles it, to at least some extent, instead of using an entirely new term. This is why I have taken *identity* for 'set of all properties' or 'complete description'. Thus, from now on in this book, wherever you find 'identity', take its definition as follows:

> At any instant, the identity of something is the set of all its properties or is its complete description.

NULL SITUATION

Regarding something, 'situation' in a physical sense is taken as 'its position with respect to or the way in which it is affected by its surroundings or by the things other than itself'. Thus, the situation in which something remains uninfluenced from everything other than itself can be termed *null situation* and denoted by S_0.

Things that are at finite distance from each other affect each other by fields such as gravitational, electric, and magnetic. So the only way for anything to remain uninfluenced from everything other than itself or to remain in the null situation is by being at an infinite distance from everything other than itself or by existing as the sole content of an infinitely large space. Thus, throughout the time something exists as the sole content of an infinitely large space, it undergoes the null situation S_0, being affected only by itself.

PRINCIPLE OF CONSECUTIVE FRAMES

In Chapter 3, I showed you that

> Immaterial of the number of times you with the same personality (likes, dislikes, capabilities, weaknesses, knowledge, experience, and so on) undergo the same situation, each time you perform the same work or action. ... (4.3)

or that

> When you with a definite personality undergo a definite situation, you perform predestined and unchangeable work or action. ... (4.4)

Observations corresponding to innumerable types of experiments performed repeatedly on innumerable types of things point invariably to the fact that the law underlying the above two statements [(4.3) and (4.4)] stands true not only for you as a human being but for every corporeal thing, whether living or nonliving, that exists, to be stated in its universal form as

> Immaterial of the number of times something undergoes the same situation for a timespan of the same length, each time it exhibits the same phenomena, events, or happenings in that timespan.

or as

> If something undergoes a definite situation for a timespan of a definite length, all the phenomena, events, or happenings that it exhibits in that timespan are predetermined and inevitable. ... (4.5)

Let the above statement (4.5) be termed *principle of consecutive frames.*

The principle of consecutive frames is followed whatever be the following three factors mentioned in its definition (4.5):

1. that which undergoes the situation
2. the situation itself
3. the timespan for which the subject undergoes the situation

For example,

Example 4.1

A ball, which is hung in a room, has the following initial identity:

I_B

1. shape: solid spherical
2. material: iron
3. weight: one kilogram
4. temperature: 1000°C (one thousand degrees centigrade)

... (4.6)

Also,

> The situation S_B that the ball undergoes in the room is described by the following two points:
>
> 1. The ball is hung in the centre of the room with the help of a two-metre-long wire that is welded to its surface and that is just strong enough to hold its weight.
> 2. The room is maintained at 25°C.
>
> ... (4.7)

The timespan for which the ball having the initial identity I_B (4.6) undergoes the above situation S_B is one hour long. In short, a one-kilogram ball with the initial temperature of 1000°C is hung in the centre of a room maintained at 25°C for a period of one hour.

Repeated experiments show that

> Immaterial of the number of times the ball with the same initial identity I_B [glowing with a temperature of 1000°C, and so on (4.6)] faces the same situation S_B [being hung in the centre of a room maintained at 25°C, and so on (4.7)] for the same timespan of one hour, each time during this period of one hour, it exhibits the same happenings in the same way.
>
> As, each time the ball radiates heat, and therefore
>
> 1. Its temperature drops.
> 2. Its glow reduces to finally vanish.
>
> Also, each time it exhibits these phenomena in the same way: after it has the temperature of 1000°C [after it has the identity I_B (4.6) or after the beginning of the period of one hour],
>
> 1. Each time it takes the same time to radiate a definite amount of heat, emits the same amount of heat in a definite time, or takes the same time to emit the same amount of heat
>
> and therefore
>
> 2. Each time it takes the same time to cool down to a definite temperature, registers the same temperature drop in a definite time, or takes the same time for the same temperature drop
>
> so that

3. Each time it cools down to the same temperature in one hour and glows with the same intensity and colour in a definite time.

... (4.8)

It follows from these observations (4.8) that

If a ball with a definite initial identity I_B [glowing with a temperature of 1000°C, and so on (4.6)] undergoes a definite situation S_B [being hung in the centre of a room maintained at 25°C, and so on (4.7)] for one hour (a timespan of a definite length), all the phenomena that it (the ball) exhibits in this timespan are predestined and unchangeable.

As, after it has the temperature of 1000°C (after it has the identity I_B or after the beginning of the period of one hour),

1. It takes predestined time to radiate a definite amount of heat, or in a definite time, it radiates predestined amount of heat.

and therefore

2. It takes predestined time to cool down to a definite temperature, or it cools down to a predestined temperature in a definite time.

so that

3. It cools down to a predestined temperature in one hour and glows with predestined intensity and colour in a definite time.

... (4.9)

This (4.9) is in perfect accordance with the principle of consecutive frames (4.5).

In the above example of the principle of consecutive frames, you saw how for a particular set of three factors mentioned in its definition (4.5):

1. the subject (that which undergoes a situation)
2. the situation undergone
3. the timespan for which the situation is undergone

all the happenings that the subject exhibits in that timespan are predestined and inevitable. In any experiment if there be a change in any of these three factors, the phenomena or the way in which the phenomena are exhibited is changed, but once again the new set of phenomena for the new set of the three factors is predestined and unchangeable, according to, nothing other than, the principle of consecutive frames (4.5). For example,

Example 4.2

If a ball having the initial identity same as that of the ball in example 4.1 [I_B—material: iron, weight: one kilogram, temperature: 1000°C, and so on (4.6)], for a timespan same as that of example 4.1 (one hour), instead of undergoing the same situation as that of example 4.1 [S_B—being hung in a room maintained at 25°C, and so on (4.7)], undergoes the null situation S_0 (see section 'Null situation'), the way in which it exhibits the phenomena in the period of one hour is now different from that of example 4.1. Since the ball now undergoes null situation (exists as the sole content of an infinitely large space and therefore remains uninfluenced from everything other than itself), it receives no radiation from anywhere else, and therefore now it experiences absolute zero (–273°C) surrounding temperature, which is extremely low in comparison to that of the room. Thus, now it radiates heat at much greater rate, to cool down much more rapidly than it did in the room. But once again

> Immaterial of the number of times the ball with the same initial identity I_B [material: iron, weight: one kilogram, temperature: 1000°C, and so on (4.6)] undergoes the same situation S_0 (null situation: situation equivalent to –273°C surrounding temperature for the ball, and so on) for the same timespan (one hour), each time, in the period of one hour, it exhibits the same phenomena in the same way.

As, once again, in this new situation,

1. Each time, after it had the temperature of 1000°C [after it had the identity I_B (4.6) or after the beginning of the period of one hour], it radiates heat in the same way.

and therefore

2. Each time its temperature drops and its glow reduces in the

same ways respectively.

... (4.10)

The above statement (4.10) implies that

If a ball with a definite initial identity I_B [glowing with a temperature of 1000°C, and so on (4.6)] undergoes a definite situation S_0 (null situation: situation equivalent to –273°C surrounding temperature for the ball, and so on) for one hour (a timespan of a definite length), all the phenomena that it (the ball) exhibits in this timespan are predestined and inevitable or unchangeable.

As, once again, in this new situation during the timespan of one hour, it radiates heat in a predestined way, and therefore

1. It cools down in a predestined way.
2. Its glow reduces in a predestined way.

... (4.11)

This (4.11) is perfectly according to the principle of consecutive frames (4.5).

SITUATION THAT THE UNIVERSE FACES

The universe comprises every corporeal thing that exists. It means that there exists nothing except the universe, and therefore there is no question of it being ever affected by anything other than itself. In other words, the universe always remains uninfluenced from everything other than itself, and since the situation in which something remains uninfluenced from everything other than itself is termed the null situation (see section 'Null situation'), it can be said that

The universe always undergoes the null situation.

THE PROOF

Recall the principle of consecutive frames (4.5):

> If something faces a definite situation for a timespan of a definite length, all the happenings that it exhibits in that timespan are predestined and unchangeable.

And as it was illustrated in examples 4.1 and 4.2, the principle is followed whatever be the following three factors mentioned in its definition (4.5):

1. that which undergoes the situation
2. the situation itself
3. the timespan for which the subject undergoes the situation

Therefore, it (the principle of consecutive frames) of course applies to the happenings that the universe (as something), always facing the null situation (a definite situation), exhibits, to give the following conclusion:

> All the phenomena that the universe (as something), always facing the null situation (a definite situation), exhibits are predestined and unchangeable. ... (4.12)

Keeping in view that the universe always faces the null situation, never faces any situation other than the null situation, or cannot face any situation other than the null situation (see section 'Situation that the universe faces'), the above statement (4.12) can also be expressed as

> All the phenomena that the universe always exhibits are predestined and unchangeable. ... (4.13)

Since

1. The events that the universe exhibits are nothing except the events that take place inside the universe.
2. In reference to the universe, 'always' is a timespan of infinite length, which comprises
   (a) the past
   (b) the present
   (c) the future
   throughout which the universe undergoes the null situation (remains uninfluenced from everything other than itself).

the conclusion [(4.12) or (4.13)] can also be stated as follows:

In the universe

1. Whatever happened in the past was predestined and inevitable.
2. Whatever is happening at present is predestined and unchangeable.
3. Whatever will happen in the future is predestined and unchangeable.

... (4.14)

The third portion of the above statement (4.14-3) can be independently stated as

In the universe whatever will happen in the future is predestined and unchangeable. ... (4.15)

Thus, along with (4.14), the above statement (4.15), which is nothing except the theorem of destiny [(4.1) or (4.2)], is proved with the help of the principle of consecutive frames.

GENERAL THEOREM OF DESTINY

Statement (4.14), which has been proved above with the help of the principle of consecutive frames, means that

Not only that

(a) Whatever will happen in the future is predestined and unchangeable.

but also

(b) Whatever happened in the universe in the past was predestined and inevitable.

and

(c) Whatever is happening in the universe at present is predestined and unchangeable.

or

Whatever happens in the universe is predestined and unchangeable. ... (4.16)

The above statement (4.16), having the same meaning as that of (4.14), which has been proved with the help of the principle of consecutive frames, extends the theorem of destiny to the phenomena, events, or happenings of the past and present as well, and therefore it (4.16) can be termed *general theorem of destiny.*

THE PAST WAS UNCHANGEABLE

It was proved along with the theorem of destiny or as a part of the general theorem of destiny in the last section that

> Whatever happened in the universe in the past was predestined and unchangeable.

This proved statement implies that

> Immaterial of the number of times any instant of the past gets revived or immaterial of the number of times the universe acquires the same identity that it had at any instant in the past, each time the same happenings will take place in it from that instant for ever.

Let me make this visual with the help of an example:

Example 4.3

Immaterial of the number of times the universe acquires the same identity as it had on 00:00 a.m. 1 January 1901 (the first instant of the twentieth century), each time it will exhibit the same happenings from that instant for ever (from 00:00 a.m. 1 January 1901 for ever). As,

- Each time World War 1; invention of the atom bomb; World War 2; bombing of Hiroshima and Nagasaki; developments in science, engineering, electronics, computers, and information technology; human exploration of space, moon, and mars; splitting up of Union of Soviet Socialist Republics and reunion of Germany; and all else that happened in the twentieth century and after that in the universe will take place in the same way (each time).
- Each time you will take birth at the same place and moment from the same parents, and each time you will lead the same life, doing

and living the same things in the same way, up to the present as well as in the future.

Somewhat as, immaterial of the number of times you start seeing a movie from a particular frame, each time you will view the same things happening in the same way in the movie from that frame to its end.

This is especially to show how inevitable, unchangeable, unavoidable, or intact were the events that happened in the universe in the past, including those that happened in your life, and how absurd is it to think about any of them that should it not have happened and about an event which did actually not happen that should it have happened.

RE-EMPHASISING THE UNCHANGEABILITY OF THE FUTURE

After the second-last section, 'General theorem of destiny', nothing is left in proving that whatever has to occur in the future is predestined and inevitable. Yet once again I want to emphasise the unchangeability of the future because, as I have already mentioned in the last chapter (Chapter 3), people who believe in and even those who trade in fate or destiny think that the future, even if it is predestined, is not absolutely unchangeable or that a change at least to some extent can be brought about in it by some or other means.

You must have heard somebody say, 'Had P been a little late as Q was, the former too would have failed in boarding the flight and would have been spared from being killed in that plane crash.' All such ifs and buts are absurd. P's being successful in getting the flight at the last moment was as predestined and inevitable as Q's being unsuccessful in getting it by being just a little late, and therefore P's being killed in that plane crash was as predestined and inevitable as Q's being spared from becoming its victim.

Always remember that not even a single bit of change can be brought about in the predestined account, course, or form of any of the events that have to occur in the future by any means. Let me prove it before you in a slightly different way.

The principle of consecutive frames (4.5) can also be stated as

> All the phenomena that something facing a definite situation exhibits in a definite timespan are predestined and inevitable. ... (4.17)

You have seen how this (4.17) is followed in the examples of the heated iron ball (examples 4.1 and 4.2).

You have also seen in example 4.2 that when the same iron ball of example 4.1, for a timespan of the same length (one hour), instead of facing the situation of the room, faces the null situation as a different situation, it exhibits different phenomena in the timespan of one hour. Though, once again, it follows the principle of consecutive frames in this new situation. This is only because the phenomena exhibited by something in a timespan of a definite length changes if the situation that it undergoes changes. It means that a way to change the predestined phenomena that the universe, as something, has to exhibit in the future (a timespan of infinite length that follows or that begins just after the present) is to change the situation that the universe has to undergo (the null situation) or to make the universe face any situation other than the null situation in the future. But since the universe can never face any situation other than the null situation (anything other than the universe can never exist or the universe can never be affected by anything other than itself), it is impossible to bring about any change in the totally predestined future. In other words, to bring about any change in the predestined course of the future is as impossible as it is to influence the universe, which comprises every corporeal thing that exists, by something that is not a part of it.

Thus, nothing can bring about any change in the predestined course of the future, or whatever has to occur in the future is predestined as well as unchangeable.

DESTINY AND LIVING THINGS

I have used the example of a ball, a nonliving thing, in the process of proving the general theorem of destiny. This must not give birth to a notion in your mind that the proved statement of the general theorem of destiny [Whatever happens (happened in the past, is happening at present, and will happen in the future) in the universe is predestined and unchangeable.] is applicable only to nonliving things of the universe, not to living things.

In Chapter 3 you saw that

> When a human with a definite personality undergoes a definite situation, she performs predestined work or action.

You can easily notice the principle of consecutive frames (4.5) underlying this statement, which governs a human behaviour involving a complicated process of decision making. This is just one of the innumerable examples, which can be cited or which you can notice around you if you try, of how it (principle of consecutive frames) is being followed by living things. By mentioning this I want to remind you that it is as true for living things as it is for nonliving things, and therefore the general theorem of destiny (4.16), which has been proved with its help, too is true for both living and nonliving things, to be stated in this reference as

> In the universe whatever occurs to or is done by both living and nonliving things is predestined and unchangeable.

Since you yourself are a living thing, whatever occurs to or is done by you (whatever occurs in your life, whether in the past, present, or future) is predestined and unchangeable, as it is with other living things.

Most people think that uncertainty and indeterminacy rule in the realm of abstract phenomena. The truth is different. It is known that

> Every abstract phenomenon is an expression of a combination of some corporeal phenomena. For example,
>
> - At any instant the thought in your mind is an expression of a complex but definite physical (electrical) and chemical interactions among various portions of your brain.
> - Increase of adrenaline level in your blood is one of a number of corporeal phenomena that are expressed together in the form of anger.

All that occurs in the universe at corporeal level is predestined and unchangeable, and since all the abstract phenomena are expressions of corporeal phenomena, every abstract phenomenon that takes place in the universe too is predestined and inevitable. So your thoughts, anger, dreams, plans, and so on are as predestined as your walking, swimming, driving, and other physical works; and all your ideas, plans, deeds, endeavours, and so on with which you think that you are making or changing your future are themselves predestined and inevitable tools to bring about what is predestined as well as inevitable.

• • •

Thus, it is proved as well as explained that

> Whatever
>
> 1. occurred in the past
> 2. is occurring at present
> 3. will occur in the future
>
> whether it is related to living things or nonliving things, including phenomena such as thoughts, ideas, plans, and feelings, is predestined and unchangeable.

This is nothing except the general theorem of destiny (4.16), and with it the theorem of destiny is also proved, to be stated here with the essence of all that has been said for it in this chapter as follows:

> Whatever has to occur in the universe in the future, whether it is related to living things or nonliving things, including abstract phenomena, such as thoughts, ideas, plans, and feelings, is predestined and unchangeable or inevitable, as impossible to change as it is to influence the universe with something that is not a part of it or as it is to make the universe not to remain itself.

5

NOTHING WILL EVER HAPPEN BEYOND DESTINY 2

We all are characters in a movie.

LET ME REITERATE THE STATEMENT OF THE THEOREM OF DESTINY, WHICH I have already discussed in Chapter 2:

> The future is predestined and unchangeable. ... (5.1)

This in detail is stated as

> Whatever has to occur in the universe in the future, whether it is related to living things or nonliving things, including abstract phenomena, such as thoughts, ideas, plans, and feelings, is predestined and unchangeable. ... (5.2)

Basically, this {the theorem of destiny [(5.1) or (5.2)] is what I have shown in 'Nothing Will Ever Happen Beyond Destiny'.

I should remind you here that I have proved the theorem of destiny in two ways, putting them in the previous chapter (Chapter 4) and this one (Chapter 5), under the headings 'Nothing Will Ever Happen Beyond Destiny 1' and 'Nothing Will Ever Happen Beyond Destiny 2' respectively, this one being a bit more advanced than the former—comparatively more broad, deep, and precise—yet, to be understood, none of them needs any type of specialisation.

The previous chapter is independent and complete in itself, whereas this one (Nothing Will Ever Happen Beyond Destiny 2) uses the basic assumptions and concepts and the examples presented in the former. Thus, I would suggest you that to thoroughly understand and get a feel of how the future is predestined, go through the preceding chapter first.

OBJECTIVE

In this chapter while proving the theorem of destiny [(5.1) or (5.2)], I shall prove that

1. (a) Not only that
   i. The future is predestined and unchangeable.

   but also

   ii. Whatever happened in the universe in the past was predestined and inevitable.

   and

   iii. Whatever is happening in the universe at present is predestined and inevitable.

   or

   (b) Whatever happens in the universe, whether it is related to living things or nonliving things, including abstract phenomena, such as thoughts, ideas, plans, and feelings, is predestined and inevitable or unchangeable.
2. To change what has to occur in the future is as impossible as it is to change what occurred in the past or to influence the universe by something that is not a part of it.
3. Immaterial of the number of times the universe acquires or be imparted the same identity as it had at any instant in the past, each time, from that instant, it will exhibit the same phenomena, events, or happenings as it exhibited in the past from that instant onwards.

Comparing the objectives of both chapters, you will find that in addition to all that was shown in the previous chapter, it is also proved here that to change the future is as impossible as it is to change the past. But the main difference between the proofs of both chapters is that the treatment here is more precise, broad, and deep.

PRINCIPLE OF CONSECUTIVE FRAMES

In Chapter 3, I showed you that

> Immaterial of the number of times you with the same personality (likes, dislikes, capabilities, weaknesses, knowledge, experience, and so on) undergo the same situation, each time you perform the same work or action. ... (5.3)

or that

> When you with a definite personality undergo a definite situation, you perform predestined and inevitable work or action. ... (5.4)

Observations corresponding to innumerable experiments performed repeatedly on innumerable types of things point invariably that the principle underlying the above two statements [(5.3) and (5.4)] stands true not only for you as a human being but for every corporeal thing (whether living or nonliving) that exists, to be stated in its universal form as

> Immaterial of the number of times something with the same initial identity (see Chapter 4, 'Identity') undergoes the same situation for a timespan of the same length, each time it exhibits the same phenomena in that timespan after its initial instant. ... (5.5)

or as

> If something with a definite initial identity faces a definite situation for a timespan of a definite length, all the happenings that it exhibits in that timespan after its initial instant are predetermined and inevitable. ... (5.6)

Let the principle underlying the above two statements be termed *principle of consecutive frames* and both these statements [(5.5) and (5.6)] be termed its *definition 1* and *definition 2* respectively.

The principle of consecutive frames is followed whatever be the following three factors mentioned in its definition [(5.5) or (5.6)]:

1. the initial identity of what undergoes the situation
2. the situation itself
3. the timespan for which the subject undergoes the situation

This was illustrated in the heated-iron-ball examples of the last chapter (examples 4.1 and 4.2). Following is its other example:

Example 5.1

The identity I_C of a pressurised-oxygen cylinder which is kept in a room and on top of which a hole has just been made is given as follows:

I_C

1. material: iron
2. shape: hollow cylindrical
3. dimensions:
   (a) external diameter: one metre
   (b) height: one metre
   (c) thickness of the walls: two inches
3. content: oxygen at twenty times the atmospheric pressure
4. description of the hole:
   (a) location: at the centre of the circular surface at the top of the cylinder
   (b) dimension: one-inch diameter
5. temperature of the cylinder and its content, oxygen: 25°C

... (5.7)

Also,

> The situation S_C that this cylinder undergoes in the room is described by the following two points:
>
> 1. The cylinder, with the hole on its top, is kept at the centre of the floor of the room.
> 2. The room is maintained at atmospheric pressure and 25°C.
>
> ... (5.8)

The timespan for which the cylinder with the initial identity I_C (5.7) faces the above situation S_C (5.8) is one hour long.

Repeated experiments show that

> Immaterial of the number of times the cylinder with the same initial identity I_C [filled with oxygen at twenty times the atmospheric pressure, having a one-inch-diameter hole that has just been made at the centre of its top surface, and so on (5.7)] undergoes the same situation S_C [being kept in the centre of a room maintained at one atmospheric pressure and 25°C, and so

on (5.8)] for the same timespan of one hour, each time, in this period of one hour after its initial instant, it exhibits the same phenomena in the same way.

As, each time, since the initial pressure of oxygen inside the cylinder is twenty times the surrounding pressure (twenty times the pressure of the room or twenty times the atmospheric pressure), the gas is ejected through the hole, and therefore the pressure inside the cylinder drops until it becomes equal to the surrounding pressure, one atmospheric pressure.

Also, each time the oxygen cylinder exhibits the above phenomena in the same way: after it has the internal pressure equal to twenty times the atmospheric pressure (after it has the identity I_C or after the beginning of the one-hour-long period),

1. Each time it takes the same time to eject a definite amount of oxygen, ejects the same amount of oxygen in a definite time, or takes the same time to eject the same amount of oxygen.

and therefore

2. Each time its internal pressure drops to the same value in a definite time, takes the same time to drop to a definite value, or drops to the same value in the same time.

so that

3. Each time the same amount of oxygen is left inside the cylinder after a definite time and, at the end of the period of one hour, its internal pressure drops to the same value.

... (5.9)

These observations (5.9) are perfectly in accordance with the principle of consecutive frames [definition 1 (5.5)]. It can be concluded from these observations that

If a cylinder with a definite initial identity I_C [filled with oxygen at twenty times the atmospheric pressure, having a one-inch-diameter hole that has just been made at the centre of its top surface, and so on (5.7)] undergoes a definite situation S_C [being kept in the centre of a room maintained at one atmospheric pressure and 25°C, and so on (5.8)] for one hour (a timespan of a definite length), all the phenomena that it (the pressurised-oxygen cylinder) exhibits in this timespan after its initial instant are predestined and unchangeable.

As after it has the internal pressure equal to twenty times the atmospheric pressure (after it has the identity I_C or after the beginning of the one-hour-long period),

1. It takes predestined time to eject a definite amount of oxygen, or it ejects predestined amount of oxygen in a definite time.

and therefore

2. Its internal pressure drops to a predestined value in a definite time or takes predestined time to drop to a definite value.

so that

3. In an hour predestined amount of oxygen is left inside the cylinder and its internal pressure drops to a predestined value.

... (5.10)

This (5.10) is in perfect accordance with the principle of consecutive frames [definition 2 (5.6)].

In the above example of the principle of consecutive frames, you saw how for a particular set of following three factors:

1. the initial identity of the subject (that undergoes a situation)
2. the situation undergone
3. the timespan for which the situation is undergone

all the phenomena that the subject exhibits in that timespan after its initial instant are predestined and unchangeable. In any experiment if any of these three factors changes, the phenomena or the way in which the phenomena are exhibited is changed, but once again the new set of phenomena for the new set of the three factors is predestined and unchangeable, according to, nothing other than, the principle of consecutive frames. You saw this in the iron-ball-example duo of the last chapter (examples 4.1 and 4.2). Here is its other example:

Example 5.2

If a cylinder having the initial identity same as that of the cylinder in example 5.1 [I_C—material: iron, shape: hollow cylindrical, outer diameter: one metre, height: one metre, thickness of walls: two inches, content: oxygen at twenty times the atmospheric pressure, temperature (of both the cylinder and its content oxygen): 25°C, a hole that is one inch in diameter has just been punched at the centre of the top surface of the cylinder, and so on (5.7)], for a timespan same as that of example 5.1 (one hour from the time it had the identity I_C or internal pressure equivalent to twenty times the atmospheric pressure), instead of undergoing the situation same as that of example 5.1 [S_C: being kept at the centre of a room maintained at one atmospheric pressure and 25°C, and so on (5.8)], undergoes the null situation [S_0: remains uninfluenced from everything other than itself or exists as the sole content of an infinitely large space (see Chapter 4, 'Null situation')], the phenomena that it exhibits now in the period of one hour after the initial instant are different from that of example 5.1.

Since the cylinder now undergoes the null situation (S_0: exists as the sole content of an infinitely large space, being unaffected from everything other than itself),

- It receives no radiation from anywhere and therefore experiences –273°C or absolute zero temperature.
- It experiences zero surrounding pressure.

Therefore, now during the period of one hour after its initial instant, it exhibits phenomena that are considerably different from those of the previous example: it ejects oxygen and simultaneously cools down at a higher rate; in subsequent stages, due to extremely low surrounding temperature (–273°C), the remaining oxygen inside the cylinder turns to liquid and then finally to solid. But once again,

> Immaterial of the number of times the cylinder with the same initial identity I_C [material: iron, shape: hollow cylindrical, outer diameter: one metre, height: one metre, thickness of walls: two inches, content: oxygen at twenty times the atmospheric pressure, temperature (of both the cylinder and its content oxygen): 25°C, a hole that is one inch in diameter has just been punched at the centre of the top surface of the cylinder, and so on (5.7)] faces the same situation S_0 (null situation: situation equivalent to –273°C surrounding temperature for the cylinder, and so on) for the same timespan (one hour), each time, in this period of one hour after the initial instant, it exhibits the same happenings

in the same way.

As, in this new situation, after it has internal pressure equal to twenty times the atmospheric pressure (after it has the identity I_C or after the beginning of the one-hour-long period),

1. Each time the cylinder ejects oxygen from its hole and loses heat from itself in the same ways respectively.

and therefore

2. Each time, in a definite timespan, the oxygen inside it acquires the same temperature and pressure respectively.

so that

3. Each time
   (a) The oxygen inside it takes the same amount of time to liquidise and to solidify respectively.
   (b) The cylinder ejects the same amount of oxygen before the remaining part of it inside turns to solid.

... (5.11)

This (5.11), which is perfectly according to the principle of consecutive frames [definition 1 (5.5)], means that

> If a cylinder with a definite initial identity I_C [material: iron, shape: hollow cylindrical, outer diameter: one metre, height: one metre, thickness of walls: two inches, content: oxygen at twenty times the atmospheric pressure, temperature (of both the cylinder and its content oxygen): 25°C, a hole that is one inch in diameter has just been punched at the centre of the top surface of the cylinder, and so on (5.7)] undergoes a definite situation S_0 (null situation: situation equivalent to –273°C surrounding temperature for the cylinder, and so on) for one hour, a timespan of a definite length, all the phenomena that the cylinder exhibits in this timespan after its initial instant are predestined and invariable.
>
> As, in the new situation, after it has the internal pressure equal to twenty times the atmospheric pressure (after it has the identity I_C or after the beginning of the one-hour-long period),
>
> 1. It ejects oxygen and radiates heat in predestined ways respectively.
>
> and therefore

2. The oxygen inside it acquires predestined temperature and pressure respectively in a definite time.

so that

3. (a) The oxygen takes predestined timespans respectively to liquidise and to solidify.
   (b) It ejects predestined amount of oxygen before the remaining part of it inside turns to solid.

... (5.12)

This (5.12) is exactly according to the principle of consecutive frames [definition 2 (5.6)].

THE DEFINITENESS OF THE PAST

Let any instant of the past be denoted by t_p.

> The universe had a definite identity at any instant of the past t_p ... (5.13)

or, keeping in view the definition of identity (see Chapter 4, 'Identity'),

> At any instant in the past t_p, the universe had a definite set of properties. ... (5.14)

It (5.14) means that at any instant in the past t_p, the universe had

1. a definite shape and size
2. definite amounts of free energy and matter contents
3. a definite number of constituents (both living and nonliving), having definite identities and configured in a definite way in the space

and so on

For example,

Example 5.3

At 00:00 a.m. 1 January 1901 (the first instant of the twentieth century),

1. The universe had
   (a) a definite shape and size
   (b) definite amounts of free energy and matter contents
   (c) a definite number of constituents (both living and nonliving), such as galaxies, stars, black holes, planets, comets, animals, humans, bacteria, plants, viruses, electrons, protons, and neutrons

   and so on
2. The constituents of the universe were configured in a definite way in space, that is, the constituents of the universe had definite locations with respect to each other. As,
   (a) The Milky Way was at a definite distance in a definite direction from the other galaxy that lay closest to it.
   (b) The sun was at a definite distance in a definite direction from any particular star.
   (c) The earth was at a definite distance in a definite direction from the moon.
   (d) Winston Churchill was at a definite distance in a definite direction with respect to Adolf Hitler.

   and so on
3. Every constituent of the universe had a definite identity. As,
   (a) The earth had a definite shape, size, mass, velocity, and so on; definite amounts of water, nitrogen, coal, iron ore, and so on; definite numbers of plants, trees, animals, and so on.
   (b) Albert Einstein had a definite weight, a definite number of hair on his scalp, a definite idea in his brain, and so on.

and so on

T_P

Let a timespan of infinite length that began at any instant of the past t_p be denoted by T_p. ... (5.15)

Further,

Being a timespan of infinite length that began at any instant of the past t_p, T_p comprises

1. the portion of the past that began at t_p and ended at the last instant of the past (the instant that lay just before the present instant)

2. the present
3. the future

... (5.16)

APPLYING THE PRINCIPLE OF CONSECUTIVE FRAMES

T_p (5.15) is a timespan of infinite length that began at t_p (any instant of the past). It means that t_p is the first instant of T_p, and therefore

> The identity that the universe had at t_p is the initial identity of the universe for the timespan T_p. ... (5.17)

Keeping this (5.17) in view and also that the universe had a definite identity at any instant of the past t_p (5.13), it can be said that

> The universe had a definite initial identity for the timespan T_p. ... (5.18)

Since the universe always undergoes the null situation (see Chapter 4, 'Situation that the universe faces'),

> It (the universe) of course faces the null situation throughout the timespan T_p [the whole length of time that began at t_p (any instant of the past)]. ... (5.19)

Putting these two facts [(5.18) and (5.19)] together,

> During the timespan T_p [whole or infinite length of time that began at t_p (any instant of the past)], the universe, with a definite initial identity (the identity that the universe had at t_p), undergoes a definite situation (the null situation). ... (5.20)

The principle of consecutive frames, which in some way governs the phenomena exhibited by a corporeal thing in a timespan of a definite length during which it undergoes a definite situation with a definite initial identity, is applicable whatever be

1. the initial identity of the subject
2. the situation itself
3. the timespan for which it undergoes the situation

The examples are 4.1, 4.2, 5.1, and 5.2. So it (the principle of consecutive frames) of course applies to the phenomena that the universe, facing a definite situation (the null situation) and having a definite initial identity for T_p (the identity that the universe had at t_p), exhibits during T_p after its initial instant. Both definitions of the principle of consecutive frames [definition 1 (5.5) and definition 2 (5.6)] can be applied to prove the theorem of destiny. The application of definition 2 proves it more directly in comparison to that of definition 1. This is why I have presented it here first.

PROVING WITH THE HELP OF DEFINITION 2 OF THE PRINCIPLE OF CONSECUTIVE FRAMES

Recall the definition 2 of the principle of consecutive frames (5.6):

> If something with a definite initial identity undergoes a definite situation for a timespan of a definite length, all the phenomena that it exhibits in that timespan after its initial instant are predestined and inevitable.

The universe, as something, with a definite initial identity [the identity that it had at t_p (any instant of the past)], for a timespan of a definite length T_p, undergoes a definite situation S_0 (null situation: the universe remains unaffected from everything other than itself) [illustrated from (5.13) to (5.20)], and therefore according to the definition 2 of the principle of consecutive frames (5.6),

> All the events that are exhibited by or that take place in it (the universe) in this timespan T_p after its initial instant t_p are predestined and unchangeable. ... (5.21)

According to (5.16),

> T_p, being a timespan of infinite length that began at any instant of the past t_p, comprises
>
> 1. the portion of the past that began at t_p and ended at the last instant of the past (the instant that lay just before the present instant)
> 2. the present

3. the future

Keeping this in view, the above conclusion (5.21) can also be stated as

In the universe

1. Whatever happened in that portion of the past that began just after any instant of the past t_p and ended at its last instant was predestined and inevitable.
2. Whatever is happening at present is predestined and unchangeable.
3. Whatever will occur in the future is predestined and unchangeable.

... (5.22)

The third portion of the above statement (5.22-3) can be independently stated as

In the universe whatever will happen in the future is predestined and inevitable. ... (5.23)

Thus, the above statement (5.23), which is nothing except the theorem of destiny [(5.1) or (5.2)], is proved with the help of the definition 2 of the principle of consecutive frames.

GENERAL THEOREM OF DESTINY

Statement (5.22), which has been proved above with the help of the definition 2 of the principle of consecutive frames, means that

Not only that

1. Whatever will happen in the universe in the future is predestined and unchangeable.

but also

2. Whatever happened in the universe in the past was predestined and unchangeable.

and

3. All that is happening in the universe at present is predestined and unchangeable.

or

> Whatever happens in the universe is predestined and unchangeable. ... (5.24)

The above statement (5.24), which has been proved with the help of the definition 2 of the principle of consecutive frames, extends the theorem of destiny to the happenings of the past and present as well, and therefore it can be termed the *general theorem of destiny*.

PROVING WITH THE HELP OF DEFINITION 1 OF THE PRINCIPLE OF CONSECUTIVE FRAMES

Recall the definition 1 of the principle of consecutive frames (5.5):

> Immaterial of the number of times something with the same initial identity undergoes the same situation for a timespan of the same length, each time it exhibits the same events in that timespan after its initial instant.

If this (the definition 1 of the principle of consecutive frames) is applied to the phenomena that the universe, which had a definite identity at any instant of the past t_p (see section 'The definiteness of the past'), exhibits during T_p (a timespan of infinite length that began at t_p), it concludes as

> Immaterial of the number of times the universe with the same identity that it had at any instant of the past t_p as its initial identity undergoes the same situation as the null situation for a timespan of the same length as that of T_p (infinite length), each time it exhibits the same happenings in that timespan after its initial instant t_p. ... (5.25)

Since the universe always faces the null situation or since the universe can never be away from the null situation (see Chapter 4, 'Situation that the universe faces'), the condition that each time the universe faces the null situation is not necessary to be mentioned in the above statement (5.25). Keeping this in view, it (5.25) can be modified as

> Immaterial of the number of times the universe acquires the same

> identity that it had at any instant in the past t_p, each time it will exhibit the same events after that instant for ever [during T_p after its initial instant (a timespan of infinite length that began just after t_p)]. ... (5.26)

The above statement (5.26), illustrated in example 4.3, implies that

> All the phenomena that takes place in the universe during T_p after its initial instant (after t_p for ever) are predestined and unchangeable. ... (5.27)

Recall (5.16):

> T_p, being a timespan of infinite length that began at any instant of the past t_p, comprises
>
> 1. the portion of the past that began at t_p and ended at the last instant of the past (the instant that lay just before the present instant)
> 2. the present
> 3. the future

Keeping this in view, the conclusion (5.27) of the statement (5.26) can also be stated as

> In the universe,
>
> 1. Whatever happened in that portion of the past which began just after t_p (any instant of the past) and ended at the last instant of the past was predestined and unchangeable.
> 2. Whatever is happening at present is predestined and inevitable.
> 3. Whatever will occur in the future is predestined and inevitable.
>
> ... (5.28)

The third portion of the above statement (5.28-3) can be independently stated as

> Whatever will happen in the universe in the future is predestined and unchangeable. ... (5.29)

As you can see, the above statement (5.29) is the theorem of destiny itself. Thus, the theorem of destiny is proved once again, now with the help of definition 1 of the principle of consecutive frames.

Statement (5.28) can also be stated as

> Whatever happens in the universe is predestined and unchangeable. ... (5.30)

This statement (5.30) is same as the general theorem of destiny. Thus, the general theorem of destiny is also proved once again, now in the form of (5.28) or (5.30) with the help of definition 1 of the principle of consecutive frames.

RE-EMPHASISING THE UNCHANGEABILITY OF THE FUTURE

Now, after the last section, 'Proving with the help of the definition 1 of the principle of consecutive frames', nothing is left in proving that whatever has to occur in the future is predestined and unchangeable. Yet once again I want to emphasise the unchangeability of the future: not even a single bit of change can be brought about by any means in the predestined account of any of the events that have to occur in the future. Let me prove it before you in a slightly different way.

It follows from the definition 2 of the principle of consecutive frames (5.6) that

> In a definite timespan, for a definite set of
>
> 1. the initial identity of what undergoes a situation
> 2. the situation
>
> all the phenomena exhibited by the subject (that undergo the situation) are predestined and unchangeable. ... (5.31)

You have seen how this (5.31) is followed in the examples of the heated iron ball (examples 4.1 and 4.2) and the examples of the pressurised-gas cylinder (examples 5.1 and 5.2).

You have also seen in example 4.2 that when the same iron ball of example 4.1 with the same initial identity, for the same time (one hour), instead of facing the situation of the room, faces the null situation as a different situation, it exhibits different phenomena in that time of one hour after the initial instant. Though, once again, in this new situation, it follows the principle of consecutive frames. You must have noticed the same thing for the gas-filled cylinder in example 5.2. This is only because the phenomena exhibited by something in a definite timespan after its beginning change if any or both of the following change:

1. the initial identity with which it (the subject) faces the situation
2. the situation

It means that

> The phenomena that the universe exhibits during T_p after t_p [a timespan of infinite length that began just after any instant of the past t_p, comprising of (1) the portion of the past that follows t_p and ends at the last instant of the past (the instant that lay just before the present instant), (2) the present, and (3) the future] can only be changed if any or both of the following be changed:
>
> 1. the initial identity of the universe for this timespan T_p or the identity of the universe at the first instant of T_p (at t_p), that is, the identity that the universe had at any instant of the past t_p
> 2. the situation that the universe undergoes, that is, the null situation
>
> ... (5.32)

There is no question of changing what has already occurred in the present and past portions of T_p. Only the phenomena that have to take place in the universe in the portion of T_p that lies in the future (the whole future) can be thought of being changed from what is predestined. Keeping this in view, if we restate the above statement (5.32), it sounds as

> The only way to bring about any change in the predestined course of the events that have to occur in the universe in the future is to change any or both of the following:
>
> 1. the initial identity of the universe for the timespan T_p, that is, the identity that the universe had at any instant of the past t_p
> 2. the situation that the universe undergoes, that is, the null situation

But since neither can the identity that the universe had at any instant of the past t_p be changed nor can the universe ever face any situation other than the null situation (nor can the universe ever be affected by anything other than itself), it is impossible to bring about any change in the totally predestined future. In other words, to bring about any change in what has to occur in the future is as impossible as it is to change the past or to influence the universe, which comprises every corporeal thing that exists, by something that is not a part of it.

Thus,

> None or nothing can bring about any change in whatever has to occur in the future.

or

> Whatever has to occur in the future is predestined as well as unchangeable.

DESTINY AND LIVING THINGS

The proved statement 'Whatever happens in the universe (happened in the past, is happening at present, and will happen in the future in the universe) is predestined and unchangeable' is as true for living things as it is for nonliving things.

In Chapter 3 you saw that when a human being with a definite personality faces a definite situation, he performs predestined work or action. You can easily notice the principle of consecutive frames (5.6) underlying this statement, which governs human behaviour involving a somewhat complicated process of decision making. This is just one of the innumerable examples, which can be cited or which you can notice around you if you try, of how it (the principle of consecutive frames) is being followed by living things. You have already seen how it is followed by nonliving things in the iron-ball examples of the last chapter and gas-cylinder examples of this chapter. By mentioning all this, I just want to remind you that the principle is as true for living things as it is for nonliving things, and therefore the general theorem of destiny [(5.24) or (5.30)], which has been proved with its help, too is true for both living and nonliving things:

> Whatever occurs to or is done by both living and nonliving things of the universe is predestined and unchangeable.

Since you yourself are a living thing, whatever occurs to or is done by you (whatever happened in the past, is happening at present, and will happen in the future in your life) is predestined and inevitable, as it is with other living things.

Most people think that indefiniteness rules in the realm of abstract phenomena to at least some extent. The truth is different: every abstract phenomenon is the expression of some or other corporeal phenomenon. As,

- At any instant the thought in your mind is the expression of a complex but definite physical (electrical) and chemical interactions among various portions of your brain.
- Increase of adrenaline level in your blood is just one of a number of corporeal phenomena that are together expressed in the form of anger.

All that occurs in the universe at the corporeal level is predestined and unchangeable (5.24), and since all the abstract phenomena are expressions of corporeal phenomena, every abstract phenomenon that takes place in the universe too is predestined and unchangeable. Thus, your thoughts, anger, dreams, plans, and so on are as predestined as your walking, swimming, driving, and other physical works.

Therefore, all your ideas, plans, deeds, endeavours, and so on with which you think that you are making or changing your future are themselves predestined and inevitable tools to bring about what is predestined as well as inevitable.

• • •

So it is proved as well as explained that

> Whatever
>
> 1. occurred in the past
> 2. is occurring at present
> 3. will occur in the future
>
> whether it is related to living things or nonliving things, including abstract phenomena, such as thoughts, ideas, plans, and feelings, is predestined and unchangeable.

which is nothing except the general theorem of destiny (5.24), and with it the theorem of destiny is also proved, to be stated here with the essence of all that has been said for it in this chapter as

All that has to occur in the universe in the future, whether it is related to living things or nonliving things, including abstract phenomena, such as thoughts, ideas, plans, and feelings, is predestined as well as inevitable or unchangeable, as unchangeable as the past or as impossible to change as it is to influence the universe by something that is not a part of it or to make the universe not to remain itself.

6

PREDICTION OF THE FUTURE

'I have the story of your whole life;
come, let me show you your future.'
'No, please don't kill my suspense;
let me enjoy the illusory independence.'

HUMAN BEINGS HAVE AN INHERENT DESIRE TO KNOW THEIR FUTURE. THIS has many reasons, responsible to different extents in different persons. The reason that predominates in most people is that they are not satisfied with their present. They have dedicated their present for a better future. They hope that what they desire lies in the future, and to confirm this they want to know their future.

In the effort of knowing their future, people resort to numerous ways, such as astrology, palmistry, and numerology. Well, after knowing that the future is predestined and unchangeable, the very first question that arises is whether the future can be predicted or not. The answer of this age-old question rests in this chapter.

NOTHING OCCURS AT RANDOM

Through Chapters 2–5, you saw that

> Whatever happens in the universe, whether it is related to living things or nonliving things, including abstract phenomena, such as thoughts, feelings, plans, and dreams, is predestined as well as unchangeable or inevitable.

It means that

> Whether it is related to nonliving things or living things and even whether it is abstract or not, no phenomenon in the universe occurs at random.

or

> Every phenomenon that takes place in the universe, whether it is related to living things or nonliving things, including every abstract phenomenon, such as every thought, idea, plan, and feeling, follows laws, the laws of nature.

Human being has always been immensely curious about nature. She has been trying hard to answer the questions posed by it, to understand its mysteries, and to solve its riddles through repeated observations and experiments; her efforts have resulted in the discovery of many of the laws being followed by many of the events taking place in the universe. These laws, the laws of nature, are being studied in various branches of science. To give a few elementary examples,

- Ice melts when its surrounding temperature exceeds 0°C. (physics)
- Sugar and salt are soluble in water. (chemistry)
- By absorbing carbon dioxide, water, and light energy, plants prepare glucose and oxygen with the help of chlorophyll. (biology)

The laws of nature that we know are embodiment of the understanding we have of the nature. They help us to penetrate further into the unknown. I am talking of the laws of nature here because their knowledge is essential for prediction of the future.

THE POSSIBILITY OF PREDICTION OF THE FUTURE

To start exploring the possibility of prediction of the future, let us take a simple everyday example of melting of an ice cube.

Suppose you take an ice cube and place it on a stand in a room that is at a temperature higher than 0°C (zero degrees centigrade). If you know the law that ice melts when its surrounding temperature exceeds 0°C, whether you know it by your own experience or by reading in a book, you can easily predict that in some time the ice cube will melt to form water.

The more your knowledge of the laws that something follows is, the more completely and accurately you can predict the phenomena that it will exhibit. For example, in this case if you know all the laws that govern the process of melting of ice (the laws that govern heat transfer and phase change), you can predict the time in which the ice cube will melt, the heat that it will absorb in this time, and so on.

The larger the ice cube, the longer the time it will take to melt. To predict the exact time it takes to melt, it is necessary to know its exact weight. This shows that the more details we know of something, the more completely and exactly we can predict the phenomena that it will exhibit.

The temperature of the room in which the ice cube is kept is an element of the situation that the ice cube faces. The higher the room temperature, the shorter the time in which the ice cube will melt. To predict the exact time in which it will melt, it is necessary to know the exact temperature of the room. This indicates that with the increase in the knowledge of the details of the situation that something faces, the completeness and accuracy with which one can predict about the phenomena that it will exhibit increases.

If we sum up these conclusions, we can say that

> The more we know about
>
> 1. the details of the subject
> 2. the details of the situation that it faces
> 3. the laws that it follows
>
> the more completely and exactly we can predict about the phenomena that it will exhibit in the future.

Hence,

> If you know the identity (the set of all the properties) that something has, the complete details of the situation that it faces, and all the laws that it follows, you can predict all the phenomena that it will exhibit in the future.

For example,

Example 6.1

A heated iron ball is hung in the centre of a room. If you know

1. the identity I_B that the ball has:
   (a) shape: solid spherical
   (b) material: iron
   (c) weight: one kilogram
   (d) temperature: 1000°C
2. the situation S_B that the ball faces in the room:
   (a) the ball is hung in the centre of the room with the help of a two-metre-long wire that is welded to its surface and that is just strong enough to hold its weight.
   (b) the room is maintained at 25°C.
3. laws followed by the ball, such as those of heat transfer

you can predict all the phenomena that the ball will exhibit in this situation in the future. As, you will be able to easily predict not only that the ball will lose heat, to cool down and to lose its glow, but the way in which it will exhibit this phenomenon. Thus, you will be able to predict

1. (a) the amount of heat that the ball will radiate in a definite time or
   (b) the time the ball will take to emit a definite amount of heat

and therefore

2. (a) the time that the ball will take to cool down to a definite temperature or
   (b) the temperature that the ball will acquire after a definite time
3. (a) the time that it will take to glow with a definite intensity and colour or
   (b) the intensity and colour with which it will glow in a definite time

and so on

The method to predict the phenomena to be exhibited by something in the future is same for everything, whether it is a single-material thing, such as the ball or the ice cube, or it is a group of things constituted by different materials, such as a pressurised-oxygen-gas cylinder. For the latter case, it is exemplified as follows:

Example 6.2

A pressurised-oxygen-gas cylinder at the top of which a hole has just been made is placed in a room. With common sense, you can predict the phenomena that the cylinder will exhibit: you can easily tell that the oxygen will escape from the hole and finally the inside of the cylinder will be at the pressure same as that of the room. But if you know

1. the identity I_C that the cylinder has:
   (a) material of the cylinder: iron
   (b) shape: hollow cylindrical
   (c) dimensions of the cylinder:
      i. external diameter: one metre
      ii. height: one metre
      iii. thickness of the walls of the cylinder: two inches
   (d) content of the cylinder: oxygen at twenty times the atmospheric pressure
   (e) description of the hole that has just been made:
      i. location: at the centre of the circular surface at the top of the cylinder
      ii. dimension: one inch diameter
   (f) temperature of the cylinder and its content oxygen: 25°C
2. the situation S_C that the cylinder faces in the room:
   (a) The cylinder, with the hole on its top, is kept at the centre of the floor of the room.
   (b) The room is maintained at atmospheric pressure and 25°C.
3. all the laws that the pressurised-oxygen-gas cylinder follows, especially those governing the flow of gasses through orifices

you will be able to predict not only all the phenomena that the cylinder will exhibit but the way in which it will do so in this situation. As, not only will you be able to predict that the oxygen will leave the cylinder and finally the inside of the cylinder will acquire the pressure same as that of the room, but you will be able to predict

1. (a) the amount of oxygen that the cylinder will eject in a definite time or
   (b) the time the cylinder will take to eject a definite amount of oxygen

and therefore

2. (a) the drop in the internal pressure of the cylinder in a definite time or
   (b) the time that the internal pressure of the cylinder will take to drop to a definite value
3. the time in which the pressure inside the cylinder will become equal to that of the room, one atmospheric pressure

In both the above examples, you saw that whatever be the constitution of the subject, knowing the identity it has, the situation it faces, and all the laws it follows, you can predict all the phenomena it will exhibit in the future. Thus,

> If you know the identity the universe has at present, the situation it faces, and all the laws it follows, you can predict every phenomenon that will take place in it in the future.

We already know that the situation the universe faces is the null situation (see Chapter 4, 'Situation that the universe faces'). It means that two other things that necessarily need to be known to predict the future are the identity the universe has and all the laws it follows. The next two sections carry the answers to the questions whether we can determine the identity of the universe at present and whether we know all the laws that the universe follows.

CAN WE DETERMINE THE IDENTITY THE UNIVERSE HAS?

At any instant the identity of something is the set of all its properties (see Chapter 4, 'Identity'). It means that at any instant the identity of something is its complete or hundred per cent description. Thus, at any instant the identity of the universe is the set of all its properties or its complete description. The description of the universe cannot be complete unless it comprises the identities or complete descriptions of all the things that constitute it. It means that to know the identity of the universe at any instant, it is necessary to know the complete description of its every constituent.

Things that constitute the universe are so large in number that it is practically impossible to determine the complete descriptions of all of them simultaneously. This is just one of the reasons the identity that the universe has cannot be determined.

At the microscopic level the universe is constituted of innumerable elementary particles, such as electrons, protons, and neutrons. An elementary particle is so small and it moves with such a high velocity that the extent to which we can be sure about its identity is negligible. Since the description of the universe cannot be complete unless it comprises the complete detail of everything that constitutes it, it is necessary to determine the identity of every elementary particle that constitutes the universe to determine the identity of the latter, but since it is practically impossible to determine the identity of even a single elementary particle, what can be said about the identities of the innumerable elementary particles that constitute the universe! Thus, the extremely small size, high velocity, and large number of the elementary particles that constitute the universe at the microscopic level is another limitation in the way of the determination of the identity of the universe at any instant.

To determine the identity that something has, it is necessary to observe it in some way. The universe is so large that we can observe only a small part of it—so small that we cannot say for sure what percentage of the whole universe it is. In other words, most of the universe is beyond our observation, and since to determine the details of something, it is necessary to observe it, it is not possible for us to determine the details of the major portion of the universe. So the unimaginably large size of the universe is also responsible for our being unable to determine its identity or its complete description at any instant.

To sum up,

> It is not possible to determine the complete description of the universe at any instant, because
>
> - It has too many constituents to be examined at the same time.
> - At the elementary or microscopic level, its constituents, the elementary particles, are too small and too quick to be looked at properly.
> - A major portion of it is too far from us to be observed.

DO WE KNOW ALL THE LAWS THAT THE UNIVERSE FOLLOWS?

By repeated observations of the phenomena that take place in the universe, we discover the laws they follow, the laws of nature. We have been able to solve a number of riddles of the universe and to find out a number of laws being followed by the phenomena that it exhibits; but the universe is still quite a mysterious place for us—there are numerous phenomena that we have yet not been able to understand. It means that

> Our knowledge of the laws of nature is not yet complete, or there are laws of nature that we have yet to discover.

Efforts are continuously being made to solve the remaining riddles of the universe. So, as time passes by, our knowledge of the laws will go on increasing. But as we solve one mystery, a few more appear, or with the increase in our knowledge, the number of unsolved riddles of the universe go on increasing. Shall we ever be able to solve all the mysteries and know all the laws that are being followed in or by the universe?

WE CAN PEEP INTO THE FUTURE

As you have already seen, to predict the totality of phenomena that the universe has to exhibit in the future, it is necessary to know

1. the complete description of the universe or the identity the universe has
2. the situation it faces
3. all the laws that are being followed in the universe, that is, all the laws of nature

We know that the situation the universe faces is the null situation, but since our knowledge about both the identity the universe has and the laws it follows is incomplete, it is not possible for us to predict all that has to occur in the future.

Although we cannot predict the future completely as well as accurately, yet with the limited amount of knowledge that we have of its identity and the laws it follows, we can of course peep into the future—we can predict the future with limited completeness and accuracy. For example,

Example 6.3

1. • Sun, moon, and earth move relative to each other. A solar eclipse is caused when the moon comes between the sun and the earth. With the help of various scientific principles, including those governing motion and energy transformation, we can predict the duration of a solar eclipse, the places where it will be observed, and whether it will be complete or partial.

   but

   • Our existing knowledge of the universe is not enough to enable us to foretell when a celestial body large enough to destroy humankind from earth will collide with it.

2. • By applying weather science to the data sent by the satellites, we can forecast weather.

but

• We cannot do this with hundred per cent correctness and accuracy.

3. • From our experience we can predict with complete surety that a plant that will come out of an apple seed in suitable conditions will be that of apple.

but

• We cannot predict the direction in which it will throw its first branch and the number of days it will take to reach the height of one metre.

4. • For a hard working and intelligent person, we can predict that he will succeed in life.

but

• We cannot foretell the exact nature and magnitude of his success (Could anyone predict for a boy who was very good at making computer programs that he would become the richest human of the world?).

Let me give you another example of the same category as that of the last one in the above example:

Example 6.4

In college you were the best student of your batch. You think that you will get a good job, but you are worried about your best friend. You inspire her to work hard, but she is careless by nature.

Both of you complete your graduation and go to a big city in search of jobs. After a month's search, you get an average job in an average firm. Two days after that, during an interview in a big concern, your friend is recognised by its human resource development manager as the younger sister of his classmate. As a result, she is appointed there at a pay scale four times higher than yours.

Actually, numerous factors besides hard work and intelligence decide the future of a person, to name just a few, her courage, contacts, appearance, speech, and health. Since we are unable to know all the factors with their correct magnitudes, weigh them against each other precisely, and correlate them properly with the happenings of the world, we cannot predict exactly about the successes and failures of a person. Our inability in this reference is just a sample of our inability to predict what has to occur in the universe in the future.

7

DESTINY AND YOU

Still
the roses smell sweet,
moon has hypnotic beauty,
mighty storms visit unalarmed,
crazy waves hit the shores.
But now
I watch,
I flow,
I fight,
I accept
unmoved.

THE FUTURE OF THE UNIVERSE IS PREDESTINED, UNCHANGEABLE, AND to a great extent unpredictable. Since you are a part of the universe, every bit of your future, including your future achievements, failures, friends, foes, joys, and sorrows and even including your future thoughts, imaginations, decisions, and so on, is predestined, unchangeable, and largely unpredictable. Thus, not only your successes and failures but your desires, thoughts, imaginations, planning, and work that back your successes; joy and ego that follow your achievements; and the sorrow that follows your failures, if they actually exist, are also predestined, inevitable, and largely unpredictable.

In your life you will get what is due to you (nothing more, nothing less) at the predestined time (not before, not after). No one can change his or anyone's destiny. Planning, discipline, hard work, perseverance, and so on, with which one thinks that he can change his or anyone's destiny, are themselves predestined and inevitable tools to bring about what is predestined and inevitable.

The spreading of the knowledge of the theorem of destiny to all may seem to be against their work and activity to most of you and even dangerous in the extreme sense to some of you, former thinking that people, knowing that they will achieve only what is due to them or predestined for them, will not work hard enough for the achievement of their goals and the latter thinking that people will just go to bed to take complete rest, waiting for their predestined achievements. There is no such possibility, because people know that work and achievements are two sides of the same coin—the more one works, the more she achieves—or in other words, generally, good achievements are in the destiny of those who also have hard work in it, and mostly people like achievements more than they like idleness and bed rest.

Now, when you know that everything that happens (happened in the past, is happening at present, and will happen in the future) is predestined and unchangeable and therefore your achievements will be only those that are due to you, will you at once become free from feelings such as tension, worry, anger, sorrow, and regret and rest in eternal peace? The feelings like tension, worry, anger, and sorrow are a part of human nature. Instead of being superficial, they are deep-rooted in human. Contrary to your belief that they grow upon you and forcibly catch hold of you, the truth is that you catch hold of them, nourish them, and use them. Thus, it will be wrong to say that the knowledge of the theorem of destiny will at once make you altogether free from these feelings, but of course it will make a difference: it will support you and soothe you when you will be in grief, anger, worry, tension, or fear, telling you that whatever happens is predestined and inevitable, and will initially save you from extreme ends. This difference, which the knowledge of the theorem of destiny will make in terms of your mental peace, will go on increasing as time passes by, as the knowledge goes deeper and deeper into your heart through your brain.

Part 3

It is the Time For You to Know God

8

AT THE DOORSTEP OF THE KINGDOM OF GOD

High birth,
particular religion,
paranormal power,
strong penance,
virtuous life,
ultimate devotion,
deep meditation,
annihilated ego?
You need none of them to know God.
Just open your eyes and come with me.

YOU HAVE BEEN HEARING AND READING ABOUT GOD SINCE YOU HAD HAD sense. Innumerable times you have thought about him. Your mind is full of questions about him: who is he? where is he? how does he look? are only a few of them. You have been told that he is the supreme being, the ruler of the whole universe, eternal, and so on. Alas! You have never been told who or what he actually is, because nobody knew the answer of this basic or central question.

Human beings have tried hard to find God, but none of their efforts met with success. Innumerable people have spent their whole lives in this mission but all in vain. At some time or the other in your life, you yourself also might have tried to find him, without succeeding in your effort. The time of such ignorance is over. God has revealed himself, and now I shall let you know him. I shall pinpoint God before you, and in this way I shall replace his hazy image that you have in your mind with a definite, clear, and distinct one.

The existence of God has always been a subject of debate and people can choose to believe or disbelieve in him, being grouped in theists and atheists. Now when I shall let you know him and his true attributes and influence, his existence will no longer remain a question of belief or disbelief and, as no one denies the sun today, from now on no one will deny him.

I should reiterate here that God, whom I am taking you to, is without any discrimination God of every being. In the same way, the knowledge of God is also for the whole humankind. You will know him irrespective of your caste, creed, community, religion, gender, social status, economic status, occupation, nature, character, and behaviour.

To lead you to the knowledge of the supreme being, neither have I devised any difficult, thorny, slippery, or crooked path for you nor shall I ask you to undergo any type of austerity or penance. To know God you just have to proceed with me with an attentive and open mind.

9

THE CONCEPT OF GOD

Greatest human,
omnipresent spirit,
infinite mind,
bearded father,
tireless potter,
almighty king,
sovereign lawgiver,
master of destiny,
benevolent sustainer,
prudent guide,
omniscient witness,
impartial judge,
kind redeemer,
mighty destroyer?

Seamless unity,
endless infinity,
limitless space,
primeval source,
first cause,
unstoppable time,
ruthless nature,
nature's law,
divine light,
sanctifying fire,
mysterious life,
loving death,

final destination,
ultimate truth?

Oh God! What is the meaning of God?

WHAT IS GOD? THIS IS THE QUESTION YOU HAVE IN YOUR MIND. THIS IS the starting point of the quest that begins now. It is said that a good start is equivalent to the accomplishment of half of the mission. So the beginning, which has to work as the foundation for the mission, should be strong and solid.

The question, what is God? is not complete in itself. When you place this question, you should certainly know what you are asking, what do you want to know, or what is the meaning with which you use 'God' in your question—is it God the barber? God, the book written by Mr M? God, the film made by Ms N? God, the house where Mr O lives? or God whom people believe to be almighty and whom they pray to and worship? Yes, of course, you want to know God whom people believe to be almighty and whom they pray to and worship. Does it mean that your question should have been, what is God who is known as almighty and whom people pray to and worship? In your question, is it enough to refer to God as one who is almighty and is prayed to and worshipped? Certainly not! God is neither just a word nor just one who is believed to be almighty and is prayed to and worshipped. God is the nucleus of innumerable beliefs, concepts, ideas, theories, notions, and stories, and unless you refer to them or keep them in mind while using 'God', your question, what is God? cannot be complete. Thus, to have meaning, solidity, and completeness in your question, you should know what 'God' means, and for that you should have a clear idea of whatever has been said and written about God.

For most part of history, God has been the central subject of religion, and therefore, naturally, it is religion where most of the material about God can be found. But the material of which religion should you refer to when you speak about God? The answer to this question lies in the answer of the question, which God do you want to realise—is it the Christian God, Hindu God, Islamic God, or God of any other particular religion, creed, or community? The answer is obvious: I am sure you are not curious about the God of any particular creed, religion, or community; the God you want to realise is the God of everyone irrespective of which religion one follows and even irrespective of whether one believes in him or not—the God of everyone, the whole world, the whole universe. Thus, while using 'God' what you are expected to know about God should be that of all the religions instead of being that of one particular religion.

There are numerous theistic religions, and if all that has been said and written about God in all the religions of the world be put together, it will form a bulk of innumerable words and pages. It is neither possible nor useful to know all that, but you should know at least the pith of what the major theistic religions of the world say about him.

But you may ask, 'Why should I be so sure about the meaning with which I am using "God"? Why should the question, what is God? be so complete? Why is it necessary to know so completely and exactly about God before knowing him?' It is necessary because the completeness and exactness with which you ask the question, what is God? or the completeness and exactness with which you know the concept of God at the beginning of your quest of God is one of the main factors that decide the completeness and exactness with which you understand, enjoy, and utilise the answer that you are about to receive or the knowledge of God that is about to be delivered to you.

Thus, to give you a good start by making your question complete and meaningful, I am giving you the universal idea or concept of the term 'God' by presenting here the nubs of what eight major theistic religions of the world—Christianity, Confucianism, Hinduism, Islam, Judaism, Sikhism, Taoism, and Zoroastrianism—say about God, which will work as the foundation and reference for your journey to his realisation.

Since God is the nucleus of the theistic religions, these nubs will also very closely give the central ideas of these religions. When you read them, observe the basic concept of every religion on God, the way any particular religion is unique or is different from others, the things that are common among all the religions, and the things about God that the majority of theists all over the world believe to be correct so that while I am taking you to him, you may not find it difficult to grasp the scenario and when I let you know him, you may be sure that what you have come to know is God himself, nothing else, and that he is the God of the whole world and the whole universe, not the God of only a particular religion, region, or community.

So here is the concept of God in the form of the nubs of what eight major theistic religions of the world say about him (presented primarily in alphabetical order and set in three groups according to the areas of their origin and similarity of their ideas, the order in a group being decided by their respective ages).

JUDAISM

God [YHWH (pronounced Yahweh): I am that I am, I will be what I will be] is one and only; unique; true; almighty, infinitely powerful, mighty, ultimately prevailing; universally and eternally sovereign, one who governs, lord, king; sovereign lord over nations of the world, all the earth, hosts, and all gods; majestic, the warrior; unrivalled, supreme being, highest; lawgiver, sovereign lord over nature, one who orders the times and seasons and puts the universe to order; sustainer, the father; eternal, everlasting; infinite, immanent; universal spirit, universal god, god of all nations, free from territorial restraints; wise, provident; source and paradigm of ethical obligation; inscrutable, mysterious, unknowable, incomprehensible; miraculous, wondrous; imageless, unimageable; divine, holy, transcendent; good, loving, caring, compassionate, benevolent, tender, living person, kind, merciful; forgiving, slow to anger; constant forgiver, ultimately forgiving, ever and always ready to forgive; rescuer; faithful to his promise; graceful, gracious; giver, giver of the Torah; responsible for both good and evil; just, righteous, chastising; wrathful, avenging; self-revelatory [by means of the rule of life he imposed on people (the Torah)]; marvellous; jealous.

Creator

Creator of all that exists: in six days God created all that exists out of nothing by his will and word alone, by saying, 'Let there be', and rested the seventh day.

Lord of history

God is continuously, immediately, and intimately present, active, and self-revelatory within the realm of human history, life, events, and actions; he is responsible for whatever political and military successes they obtain.

Continuous activity in the world

Ever present, the present one, responsible for everything: His activity is not only in the past but ongoing and continuous. He continuously, each day, renews the creation and remains actively present in it. He directly and actively participates in events of the world and human life. Except human actions, everything happens according to God.

Personal God

He always keeps a watch on his people and keeps on testing them for their faith and righteousness. He is always with the people, near them. They have direct intercourse with him.

God of Israel

Israel's ruler: out of sheer love, God chose Israel as a kingdom of priests and holy nation and the people of Israel as his witness and servant.

Lord's promise

Lord promised his people the possession of the land of Canaan and great progeny; protection, restoration, and redemption of Israel; to make them a special holy people or nation; and to set them high above other nations.

Lord's motifs

God expects that Israel will bring forth justice and knowledge to all the nations, will establish the perfect human society, and will guide human existence in the direction of the divine to let them witness his presence.

The covenant

YHWH is bound in a covenant relationship with the people of Israel in lieu of their selection, their protection, and his promises towards them, including those of redemption and perfect society. God requires the people of Israel to obey the guidance of the Torah and to fulfil their obligations and ethical responsibilities, that is, to be righteous, to be holy, to walk in the ways of God, and to have good conduct towards him and each other.

The Ten Commandments

The Ten Commandments, which are a part of the covenant between God and the people of Israel and which tell people about their moral, ethical, and religious responsibilities, were delivered to them by God through Moses at the mount of Sinai.

Liberated and protected Israel

He protects, sustains, and champions the people of Israel. God selected Moses as his apostle and commissioned him to lead Israel out of Egypt, to mediate his covenant to them, and to bring them to Canaan.

Guide

God is a teacher of human beings through the giving of instruction (the Torah), Bible, wisdom, knowledge, and understanding.

Judge

God judges everyone. He will severely punish the guilty [those who forget the lord and his laws (the Torah)], the sinner, and the wicked. He will reward and glorify the righteous and those who lovingly obey the Torah.

When the world ends, the ultimate intervention by God will take place: all the wicked throughout history will be recalled to life, will be judged, and will be doomed; all the righteous will be transformed and transported into a new world; and the creation will be totally restored.

Redeemer

As redeemer, he will enable human beings to experience the ultimate purpose of God, the perfected human society or his complete kingdom.

CHRISTIANITY

God [YHWH (pronounced Yahweh): I am that I am, I will be what I will be] is one, sole; unique; almighty, powerful, mighty with infinite power, mighty with the absolute power, omnipotent; ultimately prevailing, immutable; greatest; overwhelming; sovereign, lord, ruler, king, possessed of everlasting sovereignty; king of heaven, surrounded with a boundless realm of angels; universal, king over all the earth, God of heaven and of all of the earth, God of the nations, lord of world history; destroyer; first cause; eternal; without beginning or end, omnipresent; omniscient; holy (separate), divine, transcendent; incomprehensible—beyond human reason, experience, and conceptuality; numinous, wondrous; mystery that repels, dreadful, fearful; utterly ineffable; mystery that attracts attractive, glorious, beautiful, adorable; redeeming; blessing; good, loving, caring, sympathetic with human suffering; merciful, kind, helping, tender, forgiving; righteous, truthful; gracious; revealing, eager to reveal; wrathful, jealous, avenging; slow to anger; guide; wise; father of everyone, father of Christians, sustainer of the world; unimageable; perfect being; ultimate fact; true to his words; self-sufficient; giver of Bible; one who puts people to test.

Creator

Source of creatures, creator of all that exists: in six days God created all that exists out of nothing by his will and word alone, by saying, 'Let there be', and rested the seventh day.

Continuous activity in the world

Ever present, the present one: His activity is not only in the past but ongoing and continuous. He continuously, each day, renews the creation and remains actively present in it.

God's will prevails

Except human actions, everything happens according to God.

Governs nature

He orders the times and seasons. The continuation of the natural order and the causal chain depends on his will.

The Trinity

For Christians God exists in threefold figure: 1) creator, redeemer, father, and judge, 2) Jesus Christ, and 3) the Holy Spirit.

Lord of history

God is continuously, immediately, and intimately present, active, and self-revelatory within the realm of human history, life, events, and actions.

The Covenant

YHWH is bound in a covenant relationship with his chosen people, Christians. To his people the lord promised redemption and divine dominion. In lieu of their selection and his promises towards them, God demands them to fulfil their obligations and ethical responsibilities: to be righteous, to be holy, to walk in the ways of God, and to have good conduct towards him and each other—not merely legalistic behaviour but unconditional and undivided humanity, love, and forgiveness.

Jesus

Out of kindness to human beings, God, taking flesh from the pure virgin Mary, appeared on earth as Jesus. Jesus, the only son of God, is both God and human in a personal unity.

Through the events of Jesus' passion, sacrifice, suffering, death, resurrection, and glorification, God, the lord, as his incarnation of Jesus Christ, established the new covenant, accomplished the salvation of human beings, elevated the humble, made humankind alive, created a new humanity, destroys the works of Satan, and will arrive as judge on the earth at the end of time for the vindication and salvation of those who believe in him.

The Holy Spirit

God, as the Holy Spirit, is highly active after the ascension of Christ; guarantees the continuity of the church by establishing, revolutionising, reforming, and freshly creating laws, principles, and traditions in church history; is clearly recognisable and expressed in charismatic figures such as prophets, saints, and reformers; and reveals the spirit in the prophetic word or in the word of knowledge that becomes holy scripture.

Judge

Just, judge, God of judgment, judge of the world: He punishes the wicked and vindicates the righteous to his glory. When the kingdom of God arrives, he will judge all.

Kingdom of God

Jesus announced that the kingdom of God (salvation for everyone and divine dominion), through which the time of this present world is ended and overcome, is approaching, is on the threshold, or is in the midst of us. Turning in mercy and love to the suffering, guilty, outcast, and downtrodden, God himself, in sovereign power, as father, helper, and liberator, is in the midst of us or already now at work in a saving and liberating approach to those in bondage in the world.

Redeemer

Liberator: In the future God's rule will be fully established. He will deliver all, judge all, and lead his people to the eternal sabbath rest, a heavenly state of never-ending freedom, joy, fulfilment, and peace.

ISLAM

God (Allah) is one and only; unique; supreme being, unparalleled, exalted, without any partner, highest; great, source of all greatness; omnipotent; lord of everyone, lord of the worlds, master of everyone (Everyone and everything obeys him.); majestic, sovereign, inscrutably sovereign, the victorious, the unshaken; independent, self-sufficient (He reigns unchallenged on the whole kingdom of the heaven and the earth.); glorious; real, the truth, the real truth, the true one, the indefinable truth; sustainer, sole sustainer of all that exists, the subsisting; sole restorer of the world; the first cause; eternal, unborn, uncreated, beyond time, the first being; unlimited; bounteous; omniscient, all-informed; all-hearing, the hearer; all-seeing, the seer, the witness (He takes in all vision or watches over everything.); transcendent; subtle, unseen, inscrutable, inaccessibly mysterious, indefinable truth, inscrutably sovereign; immaculately divine; benevolent, all-loving, compassionate, protector, the benefactor; grateful; one who rewards; graceful; wise, provident; the avenger, severe in punishing, chastising for those who do not believe in his signs, formidable; rich; the praiseworthy; the living one.

Creator

In six days without getting tired, God created everything out of nothing all by himself by his sheer command 'Be.'

Perfect in his works

His creation is perfect and ordered.

Lawmaker

He has made laws according to which the heavenly bodies, such as the sun, moon, and stars, traverse predetermined paths. The behaviour of everything that exists in the universe is measured out because it is strictly governed by definite laws endowed to it by God.

Unchanging

The way in which God deals does not change with time.

Almighty

All-powerful, immaculately powerful, having limitless power, mighty, possessed of might, omnipotent: He governs everything that exists all by himself, without any partner. In the universe, including in the life of human beings, nothing happens or nothing is performed unless it is by the will of Allah. Thus, human is subservient to the divine; God's role in relation to human is that of a commander.

Architect of destiny

God determines the destiny of people.

Omnipresent

The presence of God is everywhere: He is unlimited. He is the first and the last, the seen and the hidden. Wherever one is, God is with him.

Light

Everlasting light, light over light, light of lights, pure light: He gives knowledge to everyone everywhere of everything. Things can be seen, known, and comprehended only due to him.

Guide

He is the God of guidance and shows every being, especially human, the right way. God, out of mercy, sends prophets to tell humans about himself, to guide them to the right path, to communicate the truth, and to give them knowledge. The Qur'an, the sacred scripture, which contains all the truth, is the true and uncreated word of God revealed to his messenger Muhammad, who was the last and the greatest of the series of prophets.

Merciful

All-merciful: God's mercy is boundless and it encompasses everything. He does best for human beings. He guides them to the right path. He is closest to human beings, and whenever a person in need calls him, he responds.

Forgiving

The constant forgiver: It is always possible for a sinner to repent and redeem himself by a genuine conversion to the truth. There is no point of no return, and God is always willing and ready to pardon.

Just

Judge, fair judge: God loves and rewards those who do good deeds, such as alleviating the suffering and active welfare service to the needy.

On the last day, when the world will end, the dead will be resurrected and a judgment will be pronounced on every person in accordance with her deeds. God will exalt the righteous and will severely punish the evildoers.

Without relatives

God has no relatives—he does not have any wife, son, or daughter.

TAOISM

God (Tao) is one, undivided; spontaneous, beyond distinctions; supreme master, ruler of the universe; primordial, uncreated (He existed before everything else.), beyond change, permanent; omnipresent, one who resides inside humans' minds; nameless; formless, indescribable; imperceptible, mysterious, indiscernible; unpredictable; free from any outside impression, immaculate; enlightenment.

All-inclusive unity

Everything that exists is a part of the single, undivided Tao. Anything that seems to have a separate existence from Tao is just an illusion.

Suchness

The unmanifest or the unconditioned (*tzu-jan*: the what-is-so-of-itself, the self-so) is the inner form of Tao. Spontaneity or naturalness is its fundamental attribute.

Wu and yu

Wu (not-being: the unmanifest, still, or changeless inner form of Tao) begets *yu* (being: Tao's manifest facet, which is the mother of all creation). *wu* and *yu* together form the Tao.

Yin and yang

The shaded and illuminated facets of every created thing are respectively known as yin and yang. They are pairs of complementary, interdependent principles, phases, or energies alternating in space and time, such as night and day, winter and summer.

Ch'i

Ch'i (immaterial breath or life force) is a primary creation of Tao. It plays the role of inner vital life force that performs the function of harmonising all created beings.

The cyclic process

Reversion is the function or movement of Tao. Yin gives birth to as well as returns to yang, and vice versa. This cyclic process of yin and yang, producing and reverting to each other, goes on perpetually.

Unity in diversity

In all the pulsations, multiplicity, cyclic processes, and periodical mutations and transformations, that is, in all the reversions that take place in the universe between yin and yang, the underlying undifferentiated, primordial, unchanging unity, the permanent Tao, is never lost.

Source of all that exists

Tao, in the form of nameless, latently contains the forms, entities, and forces of all beings and phenomena. He is the source of all life.

Continuous creation

Tao continuously shapes the universe and simultaneously keeps on transforming it by the alternations of yin and yang. The two phases of creation, the shaping of all beings and their transformation, are not only simultaneous but also perpetual.

Final destination of all that exists

Every manifest thing is created or breathed out by the unmanifest Tao, and when the former has reached its extreme or completed its time, it returns to or is breathed back in by the latter.

Sustainer

Life giving, source of all life, one who rears all beings: Tao is the hub of the whole universe.

How Tao acts through a person

Tao acts through a person without obstacle after he has realised emptiness in the mind by freeing himself from all obstructing notions, distracting passions, prejudices, and artificial cunning means.

CONFUCIANISM

God [Pinyin TIAN (Heaven), T'ien (Heaven), Ti (Lord), Shang-ti (Supreme

Lord)] is almighty, all-powerful; great, greatest; supreme being, supreme God, supreme lord, lord on high; ruler, supreme ruler, supreme power that rules over all spirits; supreme ancestor; grand; divine will; guardian of the physical laws of nature; law itself; master of life and death; nature; fate; one who produces and reproduces; active as well as creative; father of the king, father of everyone; destroyer; infinite, vast, all-embracing, all-pervading; the abode; sky; omniscient; all-seeing; abstract, impersonal, aloof, remote; divine; source of moral law, source of virtues in beings; kind, just; deity, most respected; wrathful.

Unity

Heaven, earth, and all other things that exist are a single thing—are without any doubleness.

Heaven's will is supreme

The will of Heaven is supreme and infallible.

Lawgiver

Heaven makes, gives, and protects principles, ordinances, and decrees, which are unceasing, profound, indestructible, all-pervading, and supreme.

The way of Heaven

Heaven's behaviour is based on constant principles. The way of Heaven is large, substantial, high, brilliant, far-reaching, long-enduring, unfathomable, and mysterious. One word that most clearly defines the way of Heaven is 'sincerity'.

Sustainer

God of people, God of crops, life affirming and life giving: Heaven has transforming and nourishing power. The sun, moon, stars, and constellations of the zodiac are suspended in Heaven, and all things are overspread and nourished by him.

Decides events

Heaven determines the actions of all beings and wealth, dignity, honour, and appointments of humans.

Predetermines events

Heaven predetermines life and death, riches and honour.

Giver

Generous, generous in giving: Heaven confers the nature, supreme virtue, and good conscience on beings. Heaven shapes the nature of humans and bestows on them the virtues, such as nobility, humanity, excellence, conscience, benevolence, and sagehood.

Protects righteousness

Heaven is the absolute upholder of righteousness, that is, moral law and cause of truth.

Judge

Heaven metes out punishments and rewards: His punishment for evil deeds take the form of all the miseries, such as misfortune for the children, calamities, and early death. All the blessings, such as protection, assistance, dignity, and high appointment, are for good doers.

Son of Heaven

Heaven selects the most virtuous man to make him the emperor, the son of Heaven, by his mandate. Since Heaven sees and hears the same as people do, the continuation of the mandate is conditioned by the continuation of the personal virtues (righteousness, benevolence, and so on) of the ruler, otherwise Heaven withdraws his mandate and passes it on to other.

Guide

Heaven raises great sages and imparts them with wisdom to instruct, enlighten, and awaken humankind.

Confucius

Confucius was a means, a prophet, through whom Heaven spread his message to the people for their welfare and awakening.

ZOROASTRIANISM

God [Ormazd, Ahura Mazda (Wise Lord)] is one; omnipotent; greatest, supreme, having no parallel; lord, greatest God, supreme God, leader of all other gods and entities that fight against evil; the only one who is worthy of being worshipped; the sovereign lawgiver, one who maintains order; sustainer of the universe and the cosmic order; the centre of nature, bounteous, beneficent spirit; the source of the alternation of light and darkness; eternal, immortal; all-wise; living spirit; true; righteous, just, undeceiving; holy.

Creator

He is the creator of the spiritual and the material world, Heaven and earth, and everything good. He created the universe and the cosmic order. Along with the other spirits, he created the seven *amesha spentas* (beneficent immortals): Spenta Mainyu (Holy Spirit), Asha Vahishta (spirit of truth and righteousness), Vohu Manah (spirit of good mind), Spenta Armaiti (spirit of faith and devotion), Khshathra Vairya (Divine Rule), Haurvatat (spirit of wholeness, integrity, perfection, health, and well-being), and Ameretat (spirit of immortality—protector and supporter of all plant life). Ahriman was created as a twin with Spenta Mainyu.

The choice

In the beginning the world became divided into the dominions of good (of truth, light, justice, and life) and of evil (of lie, deceit, darkness, and death), the former being headed by the all-wise, all-good, and beneficent Ahura Mazda and the latter, by the destructive and evil Ahriman. *Amesha spentas* (beneficent immortals), all the gods, the settled herdsmen or farmers (who care for their cattle and live in a definite social order), and so on are on the side of Ahura Mazda; and the evil headed by Ahriman are *daevas* (evil spirits) and a thieving nomad (an enemy of orderly agriculture and animal husbandry).

The good qualities represented by *amesha spentas* show the working of the deity and, at the same time, constitute the order binding the adherents of Wise Lord.

The battle

The struggle of the good spirits headed by Ahura Mazda and evil ones headed by Ahriman against each other makes up the history of the world. In order to vanquish Ahriman, Ormazd created the world as a battlefield. The total timespan of this battle is nine thousand years. Ahura Mazda and the evil spirit oppose each other by creating respectively good and bad things. Together with *amesha spentas,* Wise Lord will at last vanquish the spirit of evil. This will mark the beginning of the end of the visible world or the beginning of the last phase of creation, in which the original peace will be restored and the world will be wonderfully renewed and will be inhabited by the good, who will live in paradisiacal joy and peace.

Judge

Ahura Mazda is the sovereign lawgiver, the originator of the moral order, and the judge of the entire world.

The soul has to undergo a judgment. One who opts for the lie is condemned by the judgment of Wise Lord and must expect to continue in the most miserable form of existence. After the annihilation of Ahriman, the wicked will have to suffer for only three days, after which Wise Lord will deliver everyone.

Zoroaster

Ahura Mazda had given vision to Zoroaster and appointed him to preach the truth.

HINDUISM

God (Om, Om Tut Sut, Bruhm)[1] is one, undivided; unique, unmatched, incomparable; absolute; soul of everything—eternal, absolute, ultimate, divine soul; lord, supreme lord of all beings (the universe), king, ruler, master; one who controls everyone and everything; the God of the gods of all the worlds; valour; the supreme being, the greatest; glorious, being of great glory; adorable, revered; flawless (beyond all type of fault, shortcomings, and sin); extremely holy; marvellous; the supporter; the origin of everything that exists; eternal, imperishable, unborn, primal, most ancient, unchanging; immovable; infinite (without beginning, middle, and end); omniscient, beyond ignorance; beyond darkness; all-hearing, all-seeing, the witness; not known to anyone in complete; unmanifest, not visible to the normal eye, visible only to the divine eye; indefinable, indescribable; transcendental; goodness; the well-wisher; friend or selfless lover of all living beings; being of infinite form; truth; the knowledge, spiritual knowledge, self-knowledge; the object of knowledge, worth being realised; time; life; immortality; terrible; the dissolution, death; the mighty destroyer; the supreme abode, resort of the whole universe; righteousness; ecstasy, bliss; calm or full of peace; absolute peace; devotion; fire; the sacred syllable *om*; good and evil; consciousness; ocean; Ram[2], Krishn[3]; the cupid; intelligence, logic, memory; fame, prosperity; forgiveness; victory; fraud; resolution; silence.

God is everything

God is the only thing that exists—nothing exists except God.

The constitution of God

The existence or being of God is in two forms: animate and inanimate. The inanimate form manifests itself as mind, intellect, ego, sky, air, fire, water, and earth. The animate form is the one that sustains the whole universe. These two forms of him are together the source and destination of all that exists.

Creator

Father of everyone: under the supervision of God, mother nature creates all animate and inanimate objects; the creation merges back in the nature after a *kulp* (a period of 4.32 billion years); it is again created at the beginning of the next *kulp*; and thus the creation and destruction keeps on going.

Ultimate goal

The goal, the final destination of all that exists: All beings merge into his nature at the end of a *kulp* (a cycle of 4.32 billion years). Those who achieve God attain supreme peace and eternal abode; they do not take birth again.

Almighty

God has infinite power or boundless might. Everything is like a puppet in the hands of or like an instrument in the control of the divine.

Sustainer

Supporter and sustainer of the universe, sustainer of life: He is the supporter and sustainer of all.

One who gives the result of deeds

God fulfils the aim with which people worship him. He decides the results of the works people do.

Decides the destiny

God predetermines the events.

Omnipresent

He pervades the whole universe, permeates through inside as well as outside everything, and is near as well as far away.

Light

Light of all lights; self-luminous like the sun; source of the light that comes from the sun, the moon, and the fire: He illumines the entire creation.

Guide

God gives people the knowledge of the prudent way of work and living, and he himself follows the same way to set example.

Incarnations

Whenever virtue decreases and sin increases, God appears using his illusory power age after age to restore the virtues, to delete the sinners, and to re-establish righteousness. He has taken many incarnations. His births and deeds are divine, supernatural, and unearthly.

One who receives

The enjoyer: He is the enjoyer of sacrifices, worships, austerities, and penances.

Subtle

He is incomprehensible, imperceptible, inconceivable, and smallest of the small. He is the perceiver of all the objects of senses, though he does not have any of the sense organs. All things exist in him; yet in reality, they do not remain in him, and he does not remain in them.

Immaculate

Being subtle, the imperishable supreme self, seated in everybody, neither does anything nor becomes tainted.

Inactive

God has no duty and nothing is unobtainable for him. But to induce people to keep on performing their duties well, he shows himself to be active, yet he is not the doer.

Unattached

Although God is omnipresent and the source of everything, he is indifferent and unattached to everything—including good and bad, virtue and sin, love and hatred, and all the deeds and their fruits.

Impartial

No one is unlovable or dear to him, whether she is good or bad, virtuous or sinful, pious or impious.

SIKHISM

God is one; unique; incomparable; the truth, true, true forever (God abides in the realm of truth.); supreme being; great, greatest of all; possessed of all the virtues; unrivalled; eternal, primal, uncreated, immortal, imperishable; limitless, without beginning and end, infinite (His expanse has no limit, no boundary.); omnipresent; omniscient, all-knowing, inner knower; all-seeing; formless; invisible (None can see him.); indescribable; inaccessible, unreachable; virtuous; the pure light; immaculate, pure; transcendent; unerring, ocean of excellence, perfect; all-caring and always caring; merciful; source of life; one who annihilates all sorrow and fear; fearless; beautiful; eternally joyful; husband of the soul.

The name of God

The name of God—Sut-Kurtar (True Creator), Sut-Nam (True Name), or Wah-Guru (Hail Guru)[4]—is true, greatest, highest of high, and omnipresent. The universe is just a manifestation of his name.

Symbol of God

The symbols of God are *om* and *ik-om-kar* (one-*om*-creator).

There is nothing except God

Nothing exists except God; everything except God is false.

Creator

God has indescribable creative potency. He created three deities: the creator of the world (Bruhma[5]), the sustainer (Vishnu), and the destroyer (Muhaish[6]). He created the vast expanse of the universe, all that exists, with only one word.

Destroyer

He created the entire universe, and he himself will destroy it all.

Almighty

Every event in the universe, including in the life of any person, happens according to the will, command, or pleasure of God. All the powers vest in and have their source in him. His power holds and supports the weight of all that exists.

Sovereign

Master; lord, lord of the world, supreme lord; king, the king of kings: He does whatever he pleases; no order can be issued to him. He is the supreme master of all.

Great giver

Sole giver: His gifts are great, incomparable, and unlimited. Whatever people receive and consume—happiness, distress, deprivation, abuse, self-knowledge, salvation, knowledge of God, spiritual achievements, austere discipline, truth, goodness, soul, life, and so on—is all God's gift.

Determines the destiny

Architect of destiny: Nothing happens in the universe, including in the lives of human beings, except what God preordains.

Beyond change

He never changes; throughout all the ages, he is the same.

Incomprehensible

Inscrutable, unknowable: His greatness, his vastness, and his virtues are all inscrutable for anyone except him.

Maintains righteousness

He establishes and maintains righteousness on earth.

Just

Judge: God will impartially and truly judge all the beings based on their deeds and actions in the court where self-elect, enlightened saints assist him.

Soul is a part of God

The soul comes from God, and finally it will merge into or will be absorbed into him.

Guru Nanak

God ordered Guru Nanak to preach humankind.

• • •

This is the collection of the nucleuses of what eight major theistic religions say about God. They together give a clear and concrete idea of 'God', which will assist you throughout your way to his realisation. After you realise him, I shall let you know all that is true of all that has been presented above as them.

It is obvious that different religions have very different concepts about God—so different that it may seem that people of different religions have believed different beings to be God. The sets of epithets that different religions add to God are also not the same, but any unanimity that exists among the concepts of different religions about him can be found mostly in the sets of epithets they add to him. This unanimity exists in the form of a few key epithets added to him, such as 'almighty', 'omnipotent', 'supreme being', 'creator', and 'eternal', which are enough to show that despite the enormous dissimilarities in their theories and concepts, all the religions have believed in the same God.

Obviously, the epithets added to him by different religions form the most important portion of whatever has been said and written about him. Thus, the way to understand what the world has believed to be God is through the epithets added to him, but if you observe the epithets, as they are listed above in the nuclei of what the major theistic religions of the world say about him, you will find that the number of epithets added to him on which all the religions are unanimous are too few to give a complete picture of him. So the best way to comprehend the general concept of God in short is through the set of epithets added to him by the majority of people belonging to the theistic religions of the world, which is presented in the form of a list *L* as follows:

L

1. almighty
2. omnipotent
3. supreme being
4. ruler of the universe
5. one who governs nature
6. one who decides destiny
7. creator
8. first cause
9. eternal
10. limitless
11. omnipresent
12. omniscient
13. incorporeal
14. all-good
15. all-loving
16. kind
17. just

Not only have different religions different concepts about God, but the people of the same religion too differ largely in their beliefs and theories about him. In short, different people belonging to different religions and residing in different parts of the world have been giving different definitions of God and adding different sets of epithets to him. If the key similarity that exists among various theistic religions and creeds in the form of some of his important epithets shows that people have believed in the same God, the vast dissimilarities and contradictions that exist between them also do not keep mum. They say that whatever had been said and written about him is hypothetical or that he had never been known to anyone. In the next chapter, I shall give a proof of this and also the reason for doing so.

10

GOD HAD NEVER BEEN KNOWN TO ANYONE

Written on the pages of history with the ink of tears,
knit in the web of mystery with the chain of ignorance,
echoing with the growl of blood thirsty beasts,
weeping with the bleat of strangled innocence,
it was a long, dark, fearful, bloody night.

IF GOD HAD EVER BEEN KNOWN TO ANYONE, INCLUDING ANY ONE OF those who had ever claimed knowing, realising, or discovering him, he would have precisely defined God before people and today the whole world would have known him. But what can we say about knowing him when even his existence has yet been controversial, just a matter of belief! People can choose to believe or disbelieve in him, getting categorised in theists and atheists.

As you saw in the last chapter, throughout the world people of different creeds have been adding different sets of epithets to God; there has never been unanimity on the question of the set of epithets added to him. Besides, if you ask the theists who he is, the majority of them will answer that they do not know. Most of the remaining, instead of answering your question and pointing directly towards him, will beat about the bush, telling you the epithets about which they believe that they describe him, such as 'omnipotent', 'creator', 'omnipresent', 'omniscient', 'eternal', and 'incorporeal'. The rest of them will define him, in their own different ways, as nature, sun, destiny, their own deity, love, space, energy, zero, infinity, even themselves, and so on. In other words, even this minority of theists who claim to know him will not come out with a unanimous definition of his.

If any of the definitions of God that had ever been known to human beings were correct, the whole world would have been unanimous on it, as it is on the definition of the sun, moon, or earth, and there would have also been a universally accepted set of epithets found true to him, but the reality that has been shown above is just the opposite—the world has never been unanimous whether on any of the definitions of God or on any of the sets of his epithets. This proves that all the definitions of God that had ever been known to human beings are wrong or that God had never been known to anyone, including anyone who had ever claimed knowing, realising, or discovering him. It means all these definitions, instead of being based on knowledge, realisation, or experience of God, are hypothetical and so are the sets of epithets added to him on their basis. Therefore, whatever has been said and written about him, including by those who had ever claimed knowing, realising, or discovering him, is hypothetical, and by hearing or reading it, whatever you have known or believed about him is also hypothetical.

This has been proved before you so that

1. The firmness and rigidity with which you catch hold of whatever you have known or believed about him may decrease, resulting in the increase of your receptivity before I let you know him.
2. When I let you know him, instead of using your reason and discretion solely confined to the criterion of whatever you have known or believed about him, you would use your free reason and discretion to judge whatever I say yourself.

After I let you know him, you will be able to identify all that is true from whatever has been said and written about him, from whatever you have heard and read about him, and from whatever you have believed about him.

11

PREPARING YOU TO KNOW GOD

So many
stories told,
temples built,
candles lit,
incantations spelled,
prayers done,
oblations offered,
sacrifices made,
people deceived,
millenniums passed—
how long will you hide yourself?

THAT GOD HAD NEVER BEEN KNOWN TO ANYONE AND WHATEVER HAD been said and written about him is hypothetical, which I proved in the last chapter (Chapter 10), gives rise to numerous questions, a few of which are as follows:

If God had never been known to anyone,

1. Why and how did people start to imagine his existence?
2. Why did any person ever claim knowing him; realising him; being close to him or in contact with him; or being his relative, representative, or messenger? and how could she tell people about him?
3. What is the truth behind the claim that our holy books are his orders, words, and will?

4. How were the epithets that are commonly believed to be describing him added to him?

The answers of these questions are contained respectively by the subsequent sections of this chapter. After reading them it will not remain a mystery for you that how the soul of only some people are pious enough to bring them in contact with God, how he dictated our holy religious books, and why he, the ruler of the universe, is termed the ocean of kindness and justice, even if there is so much suffering, inequality, and injustice in this world; and then you will be ripe enough with the information you need to possess to receive the knowledge of God.

THE BEGINNING OF IMAGINATION OF GOD

Nature has always been full of questions and riddles for human being, and with the help of his wonderful mental ability, he has been successful in solving many of them after thousands of years of efforts. But even today his knowledge is far from being complete, as innumerable questions have to be answered, innumerable riddles have to be solved, and innumerable phenomena have to be understood yet. Even then, he has gained almost absolute confidence in himself and science and is full with untiring zeal to answer the remaining questions, so now when he comes across a new mystery, he says, 'Well, a time shall come when this too will be solved.'

But imagine the age thousands of years back, when almost nothing about nature was clear to human being. Full of wonders and unanswered questions, the universe, with its phenomena (nature), was in itself a big riddle for her. She used to look at nature with immense curiosity. When humans were unsuccessful in finding the answers of the majority of questions posed by the phenomena of the universe in spite of all their efforts, some people were forced to imagine that there exists some great, mysterious power who governs all of them (all the phenomena that take place in the universe: nature) or rules over the universe and who therefore is the supreme being. With the passage of time, this imagination of a few steadily took the form of deep-rooted belief of many. This belief, that there exists a great, mysterious power alias God who governs nature or rules over the universe and who therefore is the supreme being, worked as the nucleus for the process, which then started, of birth and development of innumerable stories, concepts, ideas, notions, imaginations, theories, beliefs, and so on about God.

Since human life depended largely on the mercy of nature and since God was considered having complete power over it, people started to worship him with the hope that he would be pleased by their doing so and his attitude towards them would remain favourable. For the purpose, prayers were composed in his honour. As time passed by, people developed mixed feelings of respect, fear, love, curiosity, and so on for God, and in the influence of their feelings, they added innumerable epithets to him, created a number of stories centred around him, developed theories about him, and so on. Later, as the bulk of material said and written about him increased, it became more and more difficult for anyone to trace that all of it is hypothetical and nobody knew him.

But if nobody knew God, why did any person ever claim that he knew him, was close to him, was in contact with him, or was his representative?

REASONS FOR THE CLAIM

In this section, to avoid unnecessary repetitions, I shall use 'the claim' to denote 'the claim of knowing God; realising him; being close to him or in contact with him; or being his relative, representative, or messenger'.

The majority of people who have ever lived on the earth have been theists, who believe that God has complete power over nature, rules over the universe, decides destiny, and so on. They desire the favour of God in the form of peace, longevity, health, power, wealth, and so on, and for the purpose they have always been eager to know him, to come close to him, and to communicate with him. Thus, as soon as a person made the claim (claimed knowing him; realising him; being close to him or in contact with him; or being his relative, representative, or messenger), she used to come in the limelight and people used to flock around her to know about him as well as to know the path with which they too could come close to him, come in contact with him, or communicate with him. If she were intelligent enough to pass through the interrogation of people; to appease their curiosity about God; to design long, difficult, slippery, crooked, and thorny methods for them to know him, see him, communicate with him, and so on; and to not let them know that she herself was as ignorant about him as they were, she would get everlasting respect, honour, and fame. People would take care of her subsistence and obey her in the hope that they would be able to know him, come close to him, or communicate with him with her help or in her direction, if not instantaneously, gradually, at some other day in life. Since God had never been known to anyone, it has never been very difficult for anyone to make people believe what is false and to attain her end in his name.

For convenience, from now on I shall use *K* to denote the persons about whom people believed that they knew God; were in contact with him; were close to him; or were his messenger, relative, or representative.

The main reasons, which were responsible to different degrees in different persons, for the claim (the claim of knowing God; being close to him; being in contact with him; or being his messenger, relative, or representative) of K can now be enumerated as follows:

1. Since people used to take care of the subsistence of K, one thought that he would not have to work for his livelihood if he made the claim and became successful in being established in the category of K.
2. One desired the respect, honour, and fame that K usually enjoyed.
3. God is the nucleus of the business of priests. Some of them made the claim to shine their business, and some others were compelled to do so to continue it.
4. Forced by their immense eagerness to know him, to come in contact with him, or to communicate with him, a number of persons have spent large portions of their lives in his search, undergoing various types of austerities and penances, but none of them could succeed. Many of them later made the claim to conceal that they spent their valuable time and underwent so many hardships in vain.
5. One desired to rule over people, as she knew that they used to obey K.
6. Some persons wanted to spread their own ideas aimed at social welfare in the name of God.

Whatever were the reasons for their claims of knowing him; being close to him; being in contact with him; or being his messenger, relative, or representative, in the process of answering questions of people about God, devising paths for them to realise him, giving their theories and ideas, and proving themselves true, K have preached and written a bulk of material about him, which has already been proved to be hypothetical in the last chapter.

TRUTH ABOUT THEISTS' KEY RELIGIOUS BOOKS

Every religion has a key book of its own: Avesta, Zoroastrianism; Tao-te Ching, Taoism; Sri Guru Granth Sahib, Sikhism; Bible—Judaism and Christianity; Qur'an, Islam; Geetha, Hinduism; Lun-yü, Confucianism; and so on. Many theists believe that the key book of their religion contains dictations, orders, words, and the will of God. Since God had never been known to or in contact with anyone, this belief cannot be true. Then, what is the origin of this belief? and how did our key religious books come into existence?

Most of the propagators of the existing theistic religions lie in the category of K (see the last section). From among the reasons enumerated at the end of the last section, the last one (no. 6) is mainly responsible for their claims of knowing him or being his representative. Forced by the curiosity to know him, they too had tried hard to realise him but in vain. On one hand they were curious to know him, on the other hand they had great desire as well as ideas for the welfare of people. They thought that it would be excellent for people if they followed their ideas. But why would people follow them?—they did not have the power of sword in their hands. This limitation could not fell their ambitions. Instead, it proved to be a plus point in the long term.

To solve their purpose, they claimed that they knew him or that they were his representatives, sent by him to convey his message to the people for their welfare. People drew to them in their eagerness of knowing him, coming close to him, or receiving his mercy. These propagators of religions were very intelligent persons, having great oratory power and leadership qualities. With their intelligence and oratory power, they could make people believe that their claim was correct, and with great leadership qualities, they collected a horde of followers around themselves. They preached their own ideas in his name. They preached codes of conducts that they thought would be good for their individual and social lives as words and will of God and as means to realise him along with various theories to support their own claim and cause. The existing key religious books are the collection of their ideas, theories, and codes of conducts, not the collection of the orders, words, or will of God. In fact, nothing has been dictated by him.

People in their hope of realising him are yet following the ideas and codes of conducts given by these propagators, thinking that they were dictated by God. See the wonders that faith can do: Thousands of kings have died since then, ruling for short spans of time, but the rule of the propagators of existing religions is yet not over. They are yet ruling over the hearts and minds of billions. Of course, they are kings of kings.

The knowledge of God will let you segregate the truth from all that has been written about him in your sacred religious book.

THE HISTORY OF EPITHETS BEING ADDED TO GOD

Whatever has been said and written about him is the collection of theories, beliefs, ideas, concepts, stories, and so on invented in different times by different people residing in different parts of the world. Of it, different persons are possessed with different sets (sets of knowledge and belief about him), depending upon their religion, caste, place of residence, and so on. The differences between the sets of knowledge and beliefs about him of persons belonging to different religions exist to such extents that it may seem that they believe different beings to be God. Thanks to the similarity that exists in the form of some of the key epithets added to him. Since God had never been known to anyone, people of different religions have never been unanimous on the set of epithets characterising him; yet they added to him almost the same key epithets—the only thing to show that people, irrespective of their religions, believed the same being to be God. The key epithets added to him by the majority of theists are given as follows in the list L:

L

1. almighty
2. omnipotent
3. supreme being
4. ruler of the universe
5. one who governs nature
6. one who decides destiny
7. creator
8. first cause
9. eternal
10. limitless
11. omnipresent
12. omniscient
13. incorporeal

14. all-good
15. all-loving
16. kind
17. just

The set of these epithets is important not only because it shows that people have believed in the same God but also because being the only thing fairly common among what theists of different creeds have believed about him, it is the most reliable part of whatever has been said, written, and believed about him.

If nobody knew God, how could people add these epithets to him, and that too almost the same epithets irrespective of their religions? Throughout the world the problems, desires, fears, curiosities, and so on of human beings have been basically the same. So it is not surprising that people of different times residing in different parts of the world independently started to imagine the existence of a great, mysterious power that governs nature; revered it as the supreme being alias God; and later added almost the same epithets to him. Thus, the history of epithets listed in L being added to God is almost the same for different religions and civilisations.

In section 'The beginning of imagination of God', I showed how people started to imagine God as a great, mysterious power who governs nature. Steadily, this imagination took the form of a deep-rooted belief and worked as the nucleus for the process of birth and development of innumerable other beliefs, concepts, ideas, notions, and so on about him. Therefore, from among the epithets listed in L, 'one who governs nature' (5L) was initial as well as fundamental, nuclear, or indispensable to him, and as time passed by, others too were added to him due to their own reasons.

People believed that God governs nature, that is, they believed that everything in the universe happens according to his will. Thus, naturally, he was termed the ruler of the universe (4L). And since they believed that he has complete, absolute, or unconditional authority over the universe as well as nature, they described him as almighty (1L) or omnipotent (2L).

It was believed that God has complete authority over the universe as well as nature and in this sense no one is above him or parallel to him. Thus, he was termed the supreme being (3L).

God was believed to govern whatever happens in the universe. Thus, he only was thought to govern the events that were believed to be predestined or about which people thought that they lie in the ambit of destiny. In this way, he came to be known as one who decides destiny (6L).

People believed that he governs nature or everything happens according to him and that he determines destiny. They worshipped him so that his attitude towards them would remain favourable; they hoped, desired, expected, and prayed him to be loving, kind, good, and just. Thus, God was described as all-good (14L), all-loving (15L), kind (16L), and just (17L). K [the persons about whom people have believed that they knew God; were in contact with him; were close to him; or were his messenger, relative, or representative (see section 'Reasons for the claim')] too used to assert repeatedly that he is all-good, all-loving, kind, and just to increase the faith of people in him and in this way to improve the business they conducted in his name.

People believed that K knew God, and therefore they thought that they were very knowledgeable. So they used to put before them questions for which they themselves could not find any answers in spite of all their efforts. These questions used to be of various types, such as about life, nature, cosmos, and God. To show people that they knew everything, to show them that they were different from them, to prove their specific utility in society, and to maintain their faith in them, K had to answer all these questions, whether they knew their correct answers or not. While answering any question of which they did not know the correct answer, the very first thing they used to keep in mind was that from their answers people might not know that they themselves were ignorant. In this way, K created mess from the point of view of science, which is yet being carried by the faithful.

People were always curious to know how the universe came into existence. Unable to find the answer of this question themselves, they used to ask K for it, who were also ignorant of it, but to save their position, they had to answer and that too in such a way that people might not discover their ignorance. K made the masses believe that God is the creator (7L), thinking that

1. If people believe that God is the supreme being and that everything in the universe happens according to him, it will not be difficult for them to accept that he himself is the creator.
2. Since nobody has ever seen God or the process of creation, it will be impossible for anyone to check the authenticity of this answer.

Hence, they gave birth to stories of creation of the sun, moon, earth, stars, humankind, species of plants and animals, and so on, which we find in our religious books and which science has proved false.

Curiosity knew no limits. The subsequent question was, 'If God created all this, who created him?' Now if K took the name of someone, say H, as the creator of God, people would ask innumerable questions about H, as they did about God, such as

- If H created God, why should she not be termed the supreme being?
- Who created H?

To solve this problem forever, K said, 'No one has created God. He is beyond creation. He has been for ever.' In the answer to similar questions related to the destruction of the universe, they used to say, 'God destroys the universe at his own will. He himself is beyond destruction, he will never die, he will always be present.' In this way, God came to be known as beyond creation and destruction, or eternal (9L).

Most of the questions that people asked K were of course about God. K themselves did not know God or anything about him, but they had to answer these questions to save their position. The main question about God was, who is he? K had already tried to find him out without being successful in their efforts. Now if they took the name of any existing thing, corporeal or incorporeal, as God, people would check whether it is correctly described by the epithets added to him or not and soon find out that they were being made to believe in something false. The problem was more with categorising God as a corporeal thing because everyone could perceive corporeal things. Thus, K categorised him as incorporeal (13L).

Although the problem was diluted now, it was not completely solved. The question of people remained that which existing incorporeal thing God is, and the problem was the same: if K took the name of any existing incorporeal thing, people would identify it with the epithets added to him and easily trace that they were telling them untruth. K found a clever way out of this situation. They said, 'God is an incorporeal, divine soul. You cannot perceive him, because your soul is not pious enough.' They gave them a lot of codes of conducts and said, 'Follow these codes of conducts, and when your soul becames pious enough, he will reveal himself before you.' These codes can be found in our religious books. They have nothing to do with God or his realisation. I have already explained in the last section that most of them are aimed at individual and social upliftment, welfare, and reform.

God, who, in the aforesaid way, was assigned the image of an abstract, divine soul, was also imparted a human-like image because

- God was believed to be most powerful, and because of his intelligence, a human being is stronger than any other being that can be imagined as having a soul.
- It is easiest to imagine communication with a God having a human-like image.

In this sequence, God was assigned the masculine gender because

- Human males are generally stronger than human females.
- Most of the K, who used to tell people about God, were themselves male.

This is why you find that instead of 'she' or 'it', 'he' is used for God.

Many a times people have asked, 'Where is he?' It was necessary to answer this question because people, whom K had told that they could not perceive him unless they fulfilled the conditions laid by them, believed that they could see him. Now if K pointed towards a direction and said that God is there, people would ask, 'Why in that particular direction? why not in the other?' To solve this problem, to come out of the confusion that they themselves had, and to increase the esteem of God in the minds of people, they said that God is present everywhere or that he is omnipresent (11L).

No one knew the limit of the universe, or the universe was limitless for everyone. People believed that God is omnipresent (11L). They thought that if God is present everywhere in this limitless universe, he also must be limitless (10L).

People believed that God is omnipresent and also that he governs nature. They thought that since he is present everywhere, he must know everything. Thus, he was described as omniscient (12L).

Later, people came to realise that there is a respective cause of every phenomenon that takes place in the universe; as time passes by, one thing causes another, and therefore everything today is a result of a chain or series of causes. They thought that an infinite series of causes is not possible: there must be a prime mover, an uncaused cause, or a first cause to account for the existence of the other causes. They assumed that this role of prime mover or first cause was played by God. Thus, God came to be known as the first cause (8L).

This is how the epithets listed in L, about which the majority of you think that they describe God, were added to him. Obviously, they all have been added to him as a result of imagination and hypothesis, not his real knowledge or experience. So when I let you know him, do not feel embarrassed if you find that many of them do not describe him correctly.

12

IDENTIFICATION

Birds, trees, lakes, rivers, and mountains—
I asked them all the way to God,
and finally I found him out.

At night, stars had created an image:
Infinite joy will fill my heart.
I shall be in heaven in his very form.
Surrounded by the warmth of his boundless love,
I shall write the destiny with my own pen.
Universe will roam in my expanse.
Galaxies will bow at the hint of my eyes.
No mystery will remain a mystery for me.

The light broke on a different scene:
In a chilling storm stood the naked truth;
he stared across me with his glass eyes.
My fantasies fell like aged leaves.
My ego vanished as if it never was.
The power I thought as mine was a reflection.
The freedom I felt was just an illusion.
Even my dreams were slaves to his wish!

Birds, trees, lakes, rivers, and mountains—
he ordered them all to tell me the way,
and finally he showed himself up.

A LONG TIME HAS PASSED SINCE GOD WAS FIRST IMAGINED. YOU HAVE YET been ignorant of him. In this long period of ignorance, the feeling has taken deep roots in your heart that he is beyond your intellect and senses and to realise him your soul should be holy. I have already explained in the last chapter that how and why this feeling has been cultivated in you by those about whom you believed that they knew him. Now that you know that they themselves did not know him, throw away this feeling from your heart and come with me to know him.

The existence of something is doubtful if it is not perceptible to all. If he undoubtedly exists, he must be something from what exists or what is perceptible to all. Therefore, in this chapter, when you come to know him, do not feel awkward if you find that something that exists and that is perceptible to all is God, as I am not going to talk about anything whose existence is doubtful.

To have him revealed to you, you need to take part in a process of search or identification. As you know, if someone has to be located, his identification is needed. Thus, before trying to locate God, his identification should be searched for.

WHERE TO LOOK FOR HIS IDENTIFICATION

In Chapter 10, I proved that whatever has been said and written about him is hypothetical—collection of innumerable beliefs, concepts, ideas, theories, and so on, none of which is based on real knowledge or experience of his—and unless you know him, you cannot be sure whether anything of it is true or not. Even then, it (whatever has been said and written about him) is the only available thing that seems to be of use as his identification, but if all of it is put together, it presents an indeterminate picture of God, it is not possible to conclude who he really is, or nothing that exists matches with it. It means that instead of using it all as his identification, his identification will have to be located in it: of course, the most reliable part of it must be taken as his identification. But if there is no guarantee of correctness of anything in it, how can anything in it be termed reliable? The only way out of this problem is to follow the criterion that the reliability of something as identification increases as the number of people supporting it or believing in its correctness increases. Therefore, the part of it believed by the majority of people to describe him correctly should be considered for being awarded with the role of his identification.

EPITHETS ADDED TO GOD SEEM TO HOLD A PROMISE

Different persons have different sets of beliefs about God. The similarity that exists among the beliefs about him of persons of different religions of the world is limited broadly to a set of epithets added to him. It means that the similarity is a part of the set of all the epithets added to him by the people of all religions, not that it is present in the form of the whole of latter, because even in this matter, people of different religions are not unanimous—they add somewhat different sets of epithets to him. Once again if the criterion that the reliability of something as identification increases as the number of people believing in its correctness increases be applied, it is found that the most reliable part of the set of all the epithets added to him is the set of epithets added to him by the majority of people of all the theistic religions of the world, which therefore seems to be useful now for identifying him.

Since the set of all the epithets added to him is in itself a subset of whatever has been said and written about him, the set of epithets added to him by the majority of theists across the world is the most reliable part not only of the former (the set of all the epithets added to him) but of the latter (whatever has been said and written about him). The elements of the set of epithets added to him by the majority of theists of the world, which, being the most reliable part of whatever has been said and written about him, seems to be most useful for identifying him, are listed in L, which is once more presented here as follows:

L

1. almighty
2. omnipotent
3. supreme being
4. ruler of the universe
5. one who governs nature
6. one who decides destiny
7. creator
8. first cause
9. eternal
10. limitless
11. omnipresent
12. omniscient
13. incorporeal

14. all-good
15. all-loving
16. kind
17. just

SEARCHING FOR DISTINCT EPITHETS ADDED TO HIM

When L is noticed, it is found that some of its epithets have been added to him in the same sense. For example, 'ruler of the universe' (4L) and 'one who governs nature' (5L) have been added to him to denote the same thing that every event that takes place in the universe is governed by him or that everything in the universe happens according to him.

If everything happens according to God, he himself governs the happenings that lie in the ambit of destiny. We can also say this as, if everything happens according to God, he himself decides destiny. Thus, like 'ruler of the universe' (4L) and 'one who governs nature' (5L), 'one who decides destiny' (6L) is added to God on the basis of the same belief that everything in the universe happens according to him.

The first-three epithets in L—'almighty', 'omnipotent', and 'supreme being'—are also added to God in basically the same sense as 'one who governs nature' (5L) is, to denote that he governs every phenomenon that takes place in the universe or that he has absolute power over nature or the universe.

So all these five epithets of L—'almighty' (1L), 'omnipotent' (2L), 'supreme being' (3L), 'ruler of the universe' (4L), and 'one who decides destiny' (6L)—are added to God in the same sense as 'one who governs nature' (5L) is, on the basis of the same belief that everything in the universe happens according to him or that he governs whatever happens in the universe. It means that if the epithet 'one who governs nature' (5L) be added to God, these other five epithets are automatically added to him. Thus, in L, which at present seems to be useful for identifying him, keeping these five epithets along with 'one who governs nature' (5L) is just an unnecessary repetition in reference to the search for God. Keeping this in view, L should be modified to

L_1

1. one who governs nature (ruler of the universe, one who determines destiny, almighty, omnipotent, or supreme being)
2. creator

3. first cause
4. eternal
5. limitless
6. omnipresent
7. omniscient
8. incorporeal
9. all-good
10. all-loving
11. kind
12. just

Being just a sorted out form of L, for identifying God, L_1 is equivalent to, may be as useful as, L, with the advantage of not having unnecessary repetitions.

Can L_1 be further simplified? When L_1 is observed, it is found that some epithets in it are consequential to others. For example,

Example 12.1

Changes are a part of all that happens. If God governs all the happenings, it is he who governs all the changes that take place in the universe, and therefore God himself must be beyond any change, beyond time, or eternal; whereas the vice versa cannot be said to be true, that is, it cannot be said that if something is eternal, it must also be the ruler of the universe. Thus, 'eternal' ($4L_1$) can be said to be consequential to 'one who governs nature' ($1L_1$).

In the same way, 'all-loving', 'kind', and 'just' are consequential to but not synonymous to 'all-good', because if someone is all-good, he must be all-loving, kind, and just, but the vice versa cannot be said to be compulsorily true, that is, if someone is all-loving, kind, or just, he might not necessarily be all-good.

Since 'eternal' ($4L_1$) and the last three epithets of L_1 ('all-loving', 'kind', and 'just') are consequential to but not synonymous to 'one who governs nature' ($1L_1$) and 'all-good' ($9L_1$) respectively, the former cannot be removed from L_1 to shorten or simplify it further.

DISAGREEMENT BETWEEN THE EPITHETS

If the search of God be continued with the help of L_1 now, you will find that immaterial of the amount of time and energy of the grey matter you spend on it, you cannot locate any existing thing, whether corporeal or incorporeal, to which all the epithets of L_1 can be added at the same time. In the process they present innumerable contradictions. For example,

Example 12.2

According to $1L_1$ God is one who governs nature, that is, everything in the universe happens at his discretion, and according to $10L_1$ he is all-loving. Thus, according to the former, the life of a person goes on completely in accordance with him, and according to the latter, he loves all of us, equally.

If you look around yourself, you will find that the lives of some people are blessed with abundant money, power, or fame, whereas innumerable suffer from destitution and abasement. If according to $1L_1$ he is one who governs nature, that is, if everything in the universe happens according to him, and therefore if everything in the life of any person too happens according to him, it is he who has blessed some with abundance and many others with destitution, being partial to the former, and thus 'all-loving' ($10L_1$) cannot be added to God, as one who is all-loving cannot be partial to anyone.

These contradictions show that not the whole of L_1 but only a part of it can be of use for identifying him. Since you do not know God, you cannot say for sure which of the epithets of L_1 describe him correctly. So the problem now is to find out which epithet or epithets of L_1 should be used for identifying him.

EPITHET THAT SEEMS TO BE MOST RELIABLE FOR IDENTIFYING HIM

In the last chapter, you saw how the concept of God began from the idea of a great, mysterious power that governs nature. In the course of time, it became a deep-rooted belief that there exists a great, mysterious power alias God who governs nature or rules over the universe, that is, who governs every phenomenon that takes place in the universe. This belief worked as the nucleus for the process, which then started, of birth and development of innumerable stories, concepts, ideas, notions, imaginations, theories, and beliefs about him.

Thousands of years have gone since God was first imagined, but the nucleus never shifted from that belief; that is, the belief that God is a great, mysterious power that governs nature has right from the beginning been continuously working as the nucleus of whatever has been said and written about him. Thus, the epithet 'one who governs nature' ($1L_1$) has always been the most indispensable to God. It means that if God exists, he is one who governs nature ($1L_1$)—ruler of the universe, one who determines destiny, almighty, omnipotent, or supreme being—and consequentially eternal ($4L_1$), whether or not he is creator ($2L_1$), first cause ($3L_1$), limitless ($5L_1$), omnipresent ($6L_1$), omniscient ($7L_1$), incorporeal ($8L_1$), all-good ($9L_1$), all-loving ($10L_1$), kind ($11L_1$), or just ($12L_1$). So, of the epithets listed in L_1, one that seems to be the most reliable and indispensable for identifying him is 'one who governs nature' ($1L_1$).

Thus, with the analysis of L_1, the scanning of whatever has been said and written about God for his identification comes to a turning point with the conclusion that what seems to be most reliable and therefore useful as his identification is that if he exists, he is one who governs nature [one who governs every phenomenon that takes place in the universe (almighty, omnipotent, supreme being, master of destiny, and therefore eternal)]. The effort should now be made to find him out with the help of this most concise but most reliable identification of his.

GOD

Humans have always been immensely curious about nature. They have been trying hard to answer the questions posed by it, to understand its mysteries, and to solve its riddles through repeated observations and experimentations, which has resulted in the discovery of many of the laws being followed by many of the phenomena taking place in the universe. These laws are being studied in various branches of science. To give a few elementary examples,

- Ice melts when its surrounding temperature exceeds 0°C. (physics)
- A corporeal object attracts any other corporeal object with a

gravitational force that is proportional to the product of their masses and inversely proportional to the square of the distance between them. (physics)

- Sugar and salt are soluble in water. (chemistry)
- By absorbing carbon dioxide, water, and light energy, plants prepare glucose and oxygen with the help of chlorophyll. (biology)

Human beings have of course been successful in answering innumerable questions posed by nature, yet their knowledge is far from complete. Innumerable phenomena have yet to be understood. For example, it is not yet known how a high-power homoeopathic medicine works, even if it does not contain any material trace of the medicinal substance that it represents and from which it is basically made, or when a person tries to recall something, it cannot be said with surety how long it will take for him to succeed or even whether he will succeed or not. Does this mean that the phenomena that have not yet been fully understood or those that seem to occur by chance, including abstract phenomena such as thoughts, ideas, dreams, and feelings, occur at random? No, not at all. In fact, nothing occurs at random, or whatever happens in the universe, whether it is related to living things or nonliving things, including abstract phenomena (thoughts, feelings, and so on), is governed by a set or a group of laws, the laws of nature, whether humans have yet been successful in discovering all these laws or not (see Chapter 6, 'Nothing occurs at random').

That every phenomenon that takes place in the universe is governed by a set of the laws of nature means that the group or the set that contains all the laws of nature, including those that have yet not been discovered, governs all that happens in the universe. And that the set of all the laws of nature governs every phenomenon that takes place in the universe means that it has absolute authority over nature or it is one who governs nature.

According to his identification, God is one who governs nature or one who governs whatever happens in the universe, and since the set of all the laws of nature governs the nature or governs every happening of the universe, it is God. Therefore, God is the set of all the laws that take part in governing the phenomena, events, or happenings that take place in the universe—the set of all the laws of nature. Mathematically speaking,

God = (all the laws of nature)

Are you familiar with this use of 'set?' Here set is defined as a group of similar things that belong together or are used together, for example, tea set and chess set. Thus, roughly, you can visualise your parliament as the set of all the representatives of the people of your country and your constitution as the set of all the laws used for the governance of your nation. In a similar way, God is the set of all the laws of nature.

13

WHY CAN ANY OTHER BEING NOT BE GOD?

'Why did you put life on earth?'
'I don't play with the golden sand.'
'Next!'

'What is the map of your realm?'
'Universe and much more.'
'Next!'

BEFORE THE DISCUSSION ON THE TOPIC OF THIS CHAPTER BEGINS, I WOULD point out that being a set of laws, God is neuter gender, and therefore for God, it is not appropriate to use the pronouns 'he', 'him', 'his', and 'who' and from now on, instead of using them, 'it', 'it', 'its', and 'which' or 'that' respectively should be used.

In the course of human history, a large number of beings had been defined as God, although none of them were accepted as it (as God) by the majority of people of the world—to give just a few significant examples, universe, nature, Jesus, and Ram[1]. Besides, after knowing that God is the set of all the laws of nature, one can find reasons to think of one of some other beings such as the set that contains the universe and all the laws of nature and the set that contains all the laws of mathematics and all the laws of nature as God. You can ask for any of these beings what makes them ineligible for being God. In the last chapter, I showed that God is the set of all the laws of nature, and therefore the question why anyone or anything else cannot be God is not very reasonable. Yet, for the removal of even the last traces of doubt from your mind, it is important to have a discussion on some very significant definitions of God that were or that are believed by certain groups of people or given by some well-known persons and on some such definitions that you might have conceived, seeing its definition that we concluded in the last chapter, to see why they cannot be correct.

UNIVERSE

Many a time it is mentioned in religious texts and in the preaching of prominent religious persons that God is all-pervading or omnipresent yet unperceivable. Scientists and intellectuals generally are not satisfied with this. Most of them are of the opinion that if God exists, it must be something or someone from all that exists or that is perceivable to everyone—either God is now and here or it is nowhere. Thus, many of those who are unsuccessful in finding God become atheists. Others who are not ready to deny the existence of God and also not ready to view it as omnipresent yet unperceivable think of some or other thing, corporeal or incorporeal, that exists, that is perceivable to everyone, as God. Many of this last section of people, seeing the universe causing and staging all the phenomena that take place and awed by the measure of power, order, vastness, mystery, and wonder that it has, settle on it as God. In philosophy this is categorised as a pantheistic concept of God.

The universe is defined as all the corporeal things that exist regarded as a whole. In other words, universe is the set of all corporeal things. This can also be expressed as

universe = (all the corporeal things)

Whatever corporeal thing exists is made up of energy. Thus, we can also say that the universe is the totality of the energy that exists:

universe = (all the energy that exists)

Energy keeps on taking various shapes and forms to form all the corporeal things that exist (the universe) and to cause and exhibit all the events that take place in the universe. So the universe, being made up of energy from its very microscopic to the ultimate macroscopic level, causes and exhibits all the happenings that take place.

Naturally, one can ask why the universe, which is so vast, which is so full of energy, and which causes and exhibits all the phenomena, cannot be God.

I have already shown that the nucleus of the idea of God is the belief that it is almighty, that it governs nature or that it governs the universe or all the corporeal things that exist (see Chapter 11, 'The beginning of imagination of God'). In any sense 'govern' should not be confused here with 'cause', because in most of religions of the world most people have strongly believed God to be someone having transcendence, being untouched by or other than the corporeal world, and governing the universe in the sense of deciding the course of phenomena that take place in it instead of exhibiting them or causing them physically. Thus, God must be something other than the universe, or the universe, which is corporeal and which causes and exhibits the phenomena physically, would be one of the last things to be thought of as God. Now that we have recognised God as the set of all the laws of nature, which is incorporeal or other than the corporeal universe and which governs the whole universe and all the phenomena that take place in it just according to the central beliefs of God being almighty and abstract, even the last possibility of God being the universe is eliminated.

JESUS OR RAM

In the history of humanity, there is a long list of the names of people who, because of their sheer greatness, are believed to be embodiment of or incarnation of God. For example, many Christians believe that Jesus is God, and many Hindus believe the same for Ram and Krishn[2]. Mythological, epical, and historical figures such as Buddh[3], Jesus, Krishn, and Ram do not exist at present except in the books or in the hearts of devotees, so the question whether any of them is God or not is absurd; but since at some or other time these persons might have existed and also since some persons even in the present world are believed by certain groups of people to be God, the question whether any person can be God or not still seems to be logical and needs to be addressed.

A human being is a corporeal object and is a part of the universe. All the corporeal objects, which constitute the universe, including human beings, are temporary or changing forms that the energy takes during its ever-continuing endeavour. The universe, made up of energy and working as a single entity, is itself the cause and exhibitor of all the phenomena, including whatever works, deeds, or actions someone performs, but since the universe, including whatever or whoever it contains, as well as whatever any of its content causes, acts, or does is governed by the set of all the laws of nature, it is the latter that can be said to be finally responsible for them. Thus, the same set that governs the universe, the set of all the laws of nature, is primarily responsible for the actions of any person that exists in it, whether he is good or bad, great or ordinary, and the same two beliefs—first, the nuclear belief that God governs the universe, including all that it contains, and second, the belief that God is other than the corporeal world or the universe—that show that the set of all the laws of nature is God and that reject the idea of the universe being God come up to reject or make impossible the idea of any corporeal thing contained in the universe, including any human being, being God. But this is not the only reason any human being cannot be God.

We, the corporeal things that exist in the universe, are all like waves on the surface of the sea. Somewhat in the same way as it happens with the waves, which take birth at certain instants and places on the chest of the ocean, keep on changing and moving throughout their lives, and finally die out after some time, though the water that forms them and flows through them does not, we also take birth at some instants and places in the universe, which is a vast ocean of energy; keep on changing and moving throughout our lives; and finally die, dissolve, or disintegrate some day, though the energy that forms us and flows through us does not. This is true for every corporeal thing, whether it is living or nonliving, except for the universe. In short, though the universe itself is eternal, none of the corporeal objects that exist in it is eternal.

No religion in the world has ever accepted or believed in the concept of a mortal God, which does not exist anymore or will cease to exist, or of a God that will come into existence in the future. It has always been believed by almost everyone to be immortal, eternal, ever present, beyond time, or beyond birth and death. The belief that God is eternal is so important that it can be said to be second only to the nuclear belief that it governs the universe. In fact, the belief that God is eternal is consequential to the belief that it governs the universe because if someone or something has to govern this eternal universe, it itself must also be eternal. Since the belief that God is almighty or that it governs the universe is the nuclear belief of the concept of God, if God exists, it must be one who governs the universe. And if God is the one who governs this eternal universe, it must be eternal too, so the belief that God is eternal is, a step ahead from being important, essential for the concept of God. Simply speaking, if God exists, it must be eternal, so if something is not eternal, it is absurd thinking of the possibility of it being God. This negates the possibility of any corporeal thing of the universe being God, whether it is living or nonliving, good or bad, great or ordinary. Thus, the idea of any corporeal thing constituting the universe, including any human being, being God is negated not only by the beliefs that God governs nature and is incorporeal, which negate the possibility of the universe being God, but also by the belief, which is also essential to the concept of God, that it is eternal.

Thus, it is absurd to think that Buddh, Jesus, Krishn, Ram, or any other human being—however good or great he may be—was, is, or will be God.

RULER AND RULED TOGETHER

Let the set of all the laws of nature, God, be denoted by *G*:

G = (all the laws of nature)

and the set that contains the set of all the laws of nature G and the totality of energy (the universe) be denoted by *R*:

R = [G (all the laws of nature), universe (the totality of energy)]

Energy forms the whole universe. The events that take place in the universe are all a continuous drama caused and displayed by energy scene after scene, frame after frame. Thus, all the corporeal power to form the beings and to cause and exhibit the phenomena rests with the totality of energy, the universe. It is true that whatever the universe does is in the direction of laws, but it is also true that laws alone cannot do anything, that is, cannot form anything and cannot cause and exhibit any phenomenon. When both the laws of nature and the universe come together, all this drama is staged. This gives rise to the question that instead of the set of all the laws of nature G, which has just the power to govern (which does not have the corporeal power to cause and to form) and which therefore cannot make anything happen itself, without the aid of the universe, why all the laws of nature and the universe taken together R, which has both the power to govern and the corporeal power to form the beings and to cause and exhibit the phenomena, cannot be God.

This question is as old as the very question of God. In all theistic religions as well as in all parts of the world, there have always been people who, thinking that it is not possible for an abstract God to execute its function of governance or to even exist without the existence of the corporeal world, which has the power to form and to cause, held the belief that the universe or the corporeal world is an inseparable part of God, though this belief was held by only some people, not the majority. Most of the people of the world have believed God to be untouched by the material world. For the conclusion of this age-old debate, it is well-worth analysing the possibility of R (all the laws of nature and the universe taken together) being God.

To begin with, I would say that the universe does exist and so do the laws that govern it. They exist—and they exist distinguishably. So it is meaningless to say that the abstract God or the set of all the laws that govern the universe would not exist or would be powerless without the existence of the universe.

The answer to the question that why R cannot be God depends on what and how most people have believed about God. R, the set of (a) all the laws of nature, which govern the universe, and (b) the universe, which forms every being and causes every phenomenon, is complete in itself, staging all the drama all by itself. It is eternal, but it does not govern anyone or anything else—it is self-governing. Besides, it is not simply incorporeal. I have repeatedly said that nuclear to the concept of God is the belief that God is almighty, omnipotent, supreme being, or one who governs nature. This nuclear belief is characterised by the belief of its otherness, abstractness, or transcendence, which shows that the epithets 'almighty' and 'omnipotent', which mean 'having all the powers or all possible powers', instead of being added to God in the sense of it having all the powers one can think of, including the corporeal power to cause and to form, have been added to it to denote that it has absolute power or control over nature. This is why most people have seen God as king and potter instead of the king along with his kingdom and the potter along with the clay, even if the king is powerless without his kingdom (his people, army, land, and so on) and the potter is worthless without the clay.

To conclude, the nuclear belief of God being almighty and the characteristic belief of God being incorporeal, which have been shared by the majority of people of the world, show that by most people God has been seen as one who has absolute power over nature but who is incorporeal or remains different from or untouched by it. This is what makes it possible for the set of all the laws of nature G, which has complete power over the universe but is separated from it, to be God and makes it impossible for the set of all the laws of nature and the universe taken together R, which governs itself like a kingdom but does not govern someone else like the king and which has the power to cause and form but is not separated from the corporeal world, to be God.

LAWS OF NATURE TOGETHER WITH LAWS OF ETHICS

The concept of God originated from the imagination-turned-belief that there exists a great, mysterious power that rules over the universe. The epithet 'almighty', which denotes that God rules over this vast universe all by itself, is most nuclear to its concept. Other epithets were added to it with the passage of time. In almost every civilisation, people gave a somewhat human image to God because it was easy to imagine communication with such a God and also because humans thought high of themselves. In this sequence, epithets characterising human beings, such as 'kind', 'just', 'loving', and 'good', were added to it. People who used the concept of God for their business promoted the belief of its being good (and therefore kind, loving, just, and so on) to make the idea of God pleasant and alluring for everyone—would the almighty God seem to be of any use to the public if it were not believed to be good, that is, kind, loving, just, and so on?—so as to attract more people to themselves to solve their own purposes.

As time passed by, 'good' became an important epithet of God, so important that many people started to think that it is essential for God to be good and therefore to tend to reject the idea of something being God just because it did not seem to be good. If God is almighty, its most essential attribute, it has to be responsible for whatever happens, including good and evil, love and hatred, virtue and sin; therefore, it must be beyond both good and evil instead of just being good or bad, and if it is such, is it worth being worshipped or is there any use worshipping such a God? Hence, a debate on whether God is good or not continues among philosophers and religious people from a long time, and continues the search for a God that is both almighty and good.

After I had written the book, I got an Internet connection mainly to communicate with relevant persons while trying to get it published. One day I thought to check the Web to see whether anyone else has recognised the set of all the laws of nature as God, and I was amazed to find that Adib Ben Jebara has mentioned a similar thing. In a paper named 'All things are numbers', he has mentioned the possibility of God being the set of the laws of nature and the laws of ethics.[4]

Let the set of all the laws of ethics be denoted by *E*:

E = (all the laws of ethics)

and the set of all the laws of nature and all the laws of ethics be denoted by *GG*:

GG = (G, E)
= [G (all the laws of nature), E (all the laws of ethics)]

The reason of considering GG God is thinking of it as both almighty and good—almighty because of the presence of all the laws of nature and good because of the presence of all the laws of ethics in it—because, as I said, 'good' is also considered an important epithet of God. It is worth analysing the possibility of GG being God, as it is mentioned by Jebara, but before that let us see the sense in which 'good' has been used for laws of ethics and therefore for GG.

The epithet 'good' was added to God to represent the belief of it possessing human attributes such as kindness, love, and justice. It cannot be added to the laws of ethics or laws of nature in the same sense as it was added to God, because it is absurd ascribing such human attributes to laws. The reason of using 'good' for laws of ethics is that they are in favour of or that they promote morality, goodness, and order in the society, whereas laws of nature, being the reason of whatever happens (being the reason of good and evil, moral and immoral), can be said to be beyond good and evil in this sense. The sense in which the set of all the laws of nature and all the laws of ethics GG is proposed to be good, because of having laws of ethics as its part, is also the same as the sense in which the laws of ethics are seen as good (of promoting morality, order, and goodness in the society), and this is the sense in which the epithet 'good' will be used in this section in the analysis that follows to see the possibility of GG being God.

Whatever happens in the universe, whether it is related to living things or nonliving things and whether it is thought to be good or evil, happens in the direction of G (the set of all the laws of nature). Laws of ethics are the laws chosen by human beings for maintaining order, peace, equality, morality, and so on in the society, and this choosing too happens according to the laws of nature. Different societies situated in different places have different sets of laws of ethics, though many laws are common among them. Besides, even for a particular society, some laws of ethics gain relevance and some of the others lose relevance with the passage of time. The laws of ethics are not followed as strictly as are the laws of nature. There are innumerable instances of violation of the laws of ethics, whereas the laws of nature are never disobeyed. Since everything happens according to the laws of nature, they reserve the complete authority to decide whether laws of ethics are to be followed in any particular situation or not. All the deeds of human beings that are good or moral happen according to both G and E, that is, according to both the laws of ethics and laws of nature, whereas all the human deeds that lie in the domain of evil happen according to G but against the decree of E.

There are two ways to look at the presence of the laws of ethics in GG along with the laws of nature. The first way is to consider E (the set of all the laws of ethics) just a mask or face-saving device, having no executive power, and thus to think that GG acts completely according to G (the set of all the laws of nature), and the second way is to consider that E has executive power equivalent to G and something cannot be said to be happening according to GG unless it is according to both G and E, that is, according to both the set of all the laws of nature and the set of all the laws of ethics.

The first way of thought is more logical because laws of ethics do not actually have any executive power. All the power to govern or decide whatever has to happen is vested in the laws of nature, and events happen according to them, whether the events are in accordance with the laws of ethics or not. The laws of ethics remain in GG like a mask. In this case GG, because of having laws of nature as its part, can be said to be governing all that happens in the universe and therefore can be termed almighty, but since it will also be responsible for the events that lie within the definition of evil along with those that are good, it can be said to be beyond good and evil, not just good or evil. Thus, if GG is considered acting completely according to the laws of nature, it cannot be described by the epithet 'good' in spite of the presence of the laws of ethics as its part. Not only can GG not be described as good, but also due to the presence of the laws of ethics as a part of it, which remains dormant but tells what is right and wrong, its character becomes that of one that acts against its own conscience, that is dishonest to itself, that shows and says something and does something else, or that has a dubious and fictitious character—which is against the belief that God is perfect, spotless, honest, and truthful—and therefore GG cannot be God.

The other way to see the presence of E (the set of all the laws of ethics) in GG is to consider that it has executive power equivalent to G (the set of all the laws of nature) or that something cannot happen according to GG unless it is according to both G and E. In this case, when something moral happens, it can be said to be happening according to GG because it happens in consonance with both its parts G and E, but when something evil happens, it cannot be said to be happening according to GG as a whole, because it happens according to its part G but against its other part E. It means that GG has unconditional authority over the deeds that are moral and also those phenomena of the universe that are beyond the definition of morality but its authority over evil deeds is unclear, indeterminate, and self-defying, that is, conditional. Since evil deeds, committed by human beings, are a part of whatever happens in the universe and since the authority of GG, the set of all the laws of nature and all the laws of ethics, over these happenings (evil deeds) is obscure, indeterminate, and self-defying, the authority of GG over nature is not absolute or GG is not almighty. Thus, if in GG both its elements, both G (the set of all the laws of nature) and E (the set of all the laws of ethics), are considered having decision-making or executive power, it (GG) cannot be blamed for events involving evil because its authority on evil deeds is indeterminate, and therefore it, being responsible only for events involving good and events that are beyond good and evil, can be said to be good but, not having absolute control over nature, cannot be said to be almighty. Simply speaking, if the effect of the presence of the laws of ethics in GG is seen in such a way as to make it good, GG cannot be almighty. The epithet 'almighty' (which, when added to God, denotes its absolute control over nature) is most essential to it, or whoever is God must be almighty; so if GG is not almighty, it cannot be God.

Thus, GG, which is the set of all the laws of nature and all the laws of ethics and which has been mentioned as God by Jebara, cannot be God, whether the laws of ethics that form a part of it are seen as inactive, just telling what should happen and what should not, or they are seen as taking active part in the decisions of GG, because in the former case it is almighty but fictitious and in the latter case it is not almighty and if someone has to be God, it must be almighty and at least must not be fictitious if it is not good like E or if it is not beyond good and evil like G.

Let us see the general outcome of this discussion. Since 'almighty' is the most nuclear epithet of God, it is essential for God to be almighty. Further, if someone or something is almighty, it must be responsible for both good and evil, and therefore the epithet 'good' cannot be added to it, whether to denote that it is kind, loving, just, and so on or even in the sense it was added to E, to denote that it promotes goodness, morality, peace, and harmony in the society. In short, it is essential for God to be almighty, and one who is almighty cannot be good. This is obvious with G, which I showed to be God in the last chapter and which is almighty but, instead of being good or evil, is beyond both good and evil. The vice versa is also true: one who is good cannot be almighty, and since it is essential for God to be almighty, if someone or something is good, it cannot be God. GG, for which I showed that it cannot be God, is a perfect example of this, as when it is almighty, it is fictitious instead of being good or being beyond good and evil and when it is good, it is not almighty.

ALL THE INFALLIBLE LAWS AS A WHOLE

Many laws are strictly followed or are infallible, such as the laws of nature and laws of mathematics. Laws of ethics do not lie in this category, because they are not infallible—there are a number of instances of their violation.

Let the set of all the laws of mathematics be denoted by M:

M = (all the laws of mathematics)

and the set of all the infallible laws be denoted by S:

S = (all the infallible laws)
  = [G (the set of all the laws of nature), M (the set of all the laws of mathematics), and so on]

Whatever type of law it maybe, it has the power to govern some or other thing. For example, the laws of nature govern the happenings of the universe, and the laws of mathematics govern mathematical facts, figures, and details. Since S is the set of all possible infallible laws, it has the power to govern all those things that are governed by the different types of laws that together form it. For example, it has complete authority over both the phenomena that take place in the universe and the mathematical facts because both G, the set of all the laws of nature, and M, the set of all the laws of mathematics, are parts of it.

In the last chapter, I showed that God is the set of all the laws of nature. I took you to this conclusion from the nuclear belief about God that it has absolute power over the nature or that it is almighty. 'Almighty' means 'having all the power'. Keeping this meaning in mind, one may ask that if laws have the might to govern or decide, why God, instead of being G, cannot be the set of all the infallible laws S, which seems to have all possible might or which seems to be at least mightier than the former, G, which is just the set of all the laws of nature.

The answer is not complicated at all. It is true that 'almighty' means 'having complete power' and it is the most important epithet of God, but it is also true that the sense in which it is added to God is to denote that it has complete power over the universe, as it is possessed by G, not all possible types of powers, such as the power to govern the mathematical facts along with the power to govern the universe, as they are possessed by S; and this is why God is the set of all the laws of nature G, not the set of all the strictly followed or infallible laws S.

• • •

Innumerable things, both corporeal and incorporeal, have been proposed as God. It is not possible to check the possibility of being God for each one of them. In this chapter, I have taken the cases of some important propositions and possibilities—the universe; great humans like Jesus, Krishn, and Ram; the set that contains the set of all the laws of nature as well as the universe; the set of all the laws of nature and all the laws of ethics; and finally the set of all the infallible laws—and showed why none of them can be God. These examples give enough reasons for why any being other than the set of all the laws of nature, whether it is living or nonliving and even whether it is corporeal or incorporeal, cannot be God. For example, the case of Jesus, Krishn, or Ram shows why any corporeal being that is also not ever present, such as Omega Point, hypothesised to be God by Frank J. Tipler[5], cannot be God, the case of the set of all the laws of nature together with the universe shows why any set that contains both corporeal and incorporeal things cannot be God, and the cases of the set of all the laws of nature and all the laws of ethics and the set of all the infallible laws show why anything incorporeal other than the set of all the laws of nature, such as the set that contains all the laws of nature and all the details of the phenomena that take place in the universe, cannot be God.

Thus, it is established that anything, living or nonliving, corporeal or incorporeal, other than the set of all the laws of nature cannot be God or that God is, and is only, the set of all the laws of nature.

14

THE ATTRIBUTES OF GOD

In an immense white castle
lies in deep carefree sleep
the only absolute lord,
the almighty king of kings,
the supreme god of gods,
the reason of all unknown,
the master of all known.

In its eternal dream,
the shadowless puppeteer
toys with every shadow
with invisible cords
and unspoken words,
directing the drama
on its primordial ode.

In an immense white castle
sleeps the only master known.

YOU HAVE COME TO KNOW WHAT GOD EXACTLY AND UNDOUBTEDLY IS. Now, when you know it, it will not be difficult for you to check whether anything that has ever been said and written about it is true or not. Seeing the bulk of whatever has been said and written about it, you will also not find it difficult to infer that it may take decades for anyone to check the correctness of the whole of it and then months for anyone to read the results. Most of us do not have so much time and interest. So for the segregation of truth, instead of taking the whole of it, let us take only its key portions, such as the set of epithets added to God by the majority of theists and the very basic concepts of religions about it, the former in this chapter and the latter in the next one.

As you know, the most important part of whatever had been said and written about it is the set of epithets added to it by the majority of theists of the world. For convenience in reference, it is once again listed here in the form of list L as follows:

L

1. almighty
2. omnipotent
3. supreme being
4. ruler of the universe
5. one who governs nature
6. one who determines destiny
7. creator
8. first cause
9. eternal
10. limitless
11. omnipresent
12. omniscient
13. incorporeal
14. all-good
15. all-loving
16. kind
17. just

These epithets express the attributes ascribed to God. Let us see which of these describe God correctly and therefore what the true attributes of God are.

EPITHETS TRUE TO GOD

Since God was not known to anyone, whatever epithets were added to it were hypothetical (see Chapter 11, 'The history of epithets being added to God'), yet some of them turn out to be true to it.

One who governs nature

In Chapter 12, I showed that God is the set of all the laws that take part in governing the phenomena, events, or happenings that take place in the universe—the set of all the laws of nature. Every phenomenon that takes place in the universe is governed by a particular set of the laws of nature (see Chapter 6, 'Nothing occurs at random'). Therefore, God, being the set of all the laws of nature, governs all the phenomena that takes place in the universe or governs the nature (5L).

Ruler of the universe

God governs every phenomenon that takes place in the universe, or everything in the universe happens according to it. Thus, none other than it is the ruler of the universe (4L).

Almighty, omnipotent

God exercises complete authority over the universe and nature. In this sense, it is almighty (1L) or omnipotent (2L).

Supreme being

Whatever happens in the universe is governed by God, and since whatever happens in the universe includes whatever happens to and whatever is done by every living and nonliving thing that exists in the universe, it is God that governs every living and nonliving thing that exists. In this sense, God is above every living and nonliving thing that exists and therefore is rightly termed the supreme being (3L).

Master of destiny

Whatever happens (happened in the past, is happening at present, and will happen in the future) in the universe is

1. predestined and unchangeable (see Part 2, Chapters 2–5).
2. governed by the laws of nature (see Chapter 6, 'Nothing occurs at random').

It means that all the laws of nature put together, God, predetermines all that happens in the universe. And since predetermined or predestined course of happenings is nothing but destiny, it is God that decides the destiny of the universe and therefore of every living and nonliving thing that it contains (6L).

Incorporeal

Laws are incorporeal. Therefore, God, a set of laws, is also incorporeal (13L).

Eternal

Scientists discover the laws of nature; they do not give birth to them. They have always been present, taking part in the governance of the universe, before being discovered by the scientists. After the destruction of human beings, when there will be no one to study the laws, they will not die. They will be present for ever, governing the universe. I want to say that the laws of nature are beyond birth, death, or any type of change or that they are eternal, and since God is the set of all the laws of nature, it too is eternal (9L).

EPITHETS NOT TRUE TO GOD

Since the epithets were added to it hypothetically—in the effort to answer the questions posed by nature, to emphasise the greatness of God, and so on—most of them are not true to it.

Creator

As far as it is known to human beings, the universe is beyond creation and destruction or is eternal. Therefore, it is absurd to term anyone, including God, its creator (7L).

First cause

Every phenomenon has some cause. As time passes by, one thing causes another, and therefore everything today is a result of a chain or series of causes. According to the hypothesis of first cause, an infinite series of causes is most unlikely; there must be some first cause, some prime mover, or some uncaused cause responsible for all other causes.

Our knowledge about the universe and the phenomena that take place in it is yet incomplete. We are yet unaware of anything that plays the aforesaid role of first cause. For the time being, let us suppose that there exists an uncaused cause or a first cause that acts as a prime mover to account for the existence of all other causes. Incorporeal things cannot cause any phenomenon all by themselves. Only a corporeal thing can act as a cause for the phenomena, whether superficially or originally. It means that if it exists, the first cause has definitely some physical or corporeal existence. Since God, being a set of incorporeal laws, has no corporeal existence, neither can it be the first cause (8L) nor can the first cause be God.

According to the hypothesis of first cause, everything is originally caused by the first cause whatever may be its superficial cause. What remains in its place is that everything happens according to God. It means that the first cause originally causes everything to happen but exclusively according to God, or in the execution of its functions, the first cause, whatever it may be, is governed by God.

Limitless

Being the set of all the laws of nature, God does not lie in the category of things that have spread in space, for which 'limit' or 'bound' has any relevance. So it is absurd to add the epithet 'limitless' or 'boundless' (10L) to God.

In this reference, it is worth giving thought whether the number of laws that together form God is limitless or not. The types of phenomena that take place in the universe are innumerable but not infinite in number. Thus, the laws that govern them, which together form God, can be innumerable but cannot be infinite or limitless in number.

One may think that the universe is limitless, but according to the assessment of scientists, it has finite dimensions at any instant—it is never limitless. The only limitless thing is free space. Free space and God are related in such a way that the only thing that free space contains, the universe, is governed by God.

Omnipresent

Presence in three dimensions of space is peculiar to corporeal things, so it is absurd talking of presence in space for any incorporeal thing. Since God is incorporeal, it is absurd to describe it as omnipresent (11L).

The universe is made up of energy, which exists 'condensed' in the form of matter, made up of elementary particles, and freely in the form of light, made up of photons. In other words, the universe is made up of innumerable elementary particles and photons, which are distributed in free space. Where a particle or a photon exists, free space does not, and where free space exists, particle or photon does not. It means that neither free space nor energy, which exists in the form of elementary particles and photons, is present everywhere. Nothing corporeal except energy is present in space, and since neither energy nor free space is present everywhere, nothing is present everywhere or nothing is omnipresent (11L).

Omniscient, all-loving, kind, just

Knowledge, love, kindness, and justice are peculiar to living things. Being a set of laws, God is an incorporeal thing, far from being a living thing, so it is absurd to describe it as omniscient (12L), all-loving (15L), kind (16L), or just (17L). It is beyond love, kindness, justice, morality, virtue, sin, happiness, woe, and so on.

All-good

The epithet 'all-good' was added to God in the same sense as it can be added to any human being, that is, to denote that it is all-loving, kind, just, and so on. Since it, instead of being a human being or even a living being, is a set of incorporeal laws, it is absurd to describe it as loving, kind, just, and so on, and therefore it is absurd to describe it as all-good (14L) too.

Being the set of all the laws of nature, God brings order and predictability in the universe, and therefore it can be said to be beneficial. We also term something good when it is beneficial, and since God is beneficial, it can be termed good. Thus, though God cannot be termed all-good, it can be termed good in a particular sense: it brings order and predictability everywhere in the universe.

No living being is omniscient. A person can be loving, kind, just, or all-good but only if God allows. Since God rules over the universe or all the living and nonliving things that exist, it governs all of us, including those who are good in any sense and even those who are all-good.

ATTRIBUTES OF GOD

The important attributes ascribed to God by theists, including most of those expressed by its epithets listed in L, are unity, truth, omnipotence, supremacy, sovereignty, predestination, creativity, eternity, immutability, infinity, omnipresence, omniscience, abstractness, incomprehensibility, generosity, wisdom, goodness, love, kindness, justice, sincerity, spontaneity, aloofness, and self-sufficiency. As you have seen, being the set of all the laws of nature, God is almighty, omnipotent, supreme being, ruler of the universe, one who governs the nature, one who decides the destiny, eternal, and incorporeal, absurdly described as creator, first cause, limitless, omnipresent, omniscient, all-good, all-loving, kind, and just. Thus, of the attributes mentioned above, those possessed by God are unity, truth, omnipotence, supremacy, sovereignty, predestination, eternity, immutability, abstractness, spontaneity, aloofness, and self-sufficiency and those absurd to be ascribed to it are creativity, infinity, omnipresence, omniscience, incomprehensibility, generosity, wisdom, goodness, love, kindness, justice, and sincerity.

SUMMARY

To summarise this chapter,

1. God is
    - almighty
    - omnipotent
    - supreme being
    - ruler of the universe
    - one who governs nature
    - one who decides destiny
    - eternal
    - incorporeal
2. It is absurd to add the following epithets to God:
    - creator
    - first cause
    - limitless
    - omnipresent
    - omniscient
    - all-good

all-loving
kind
just

3. No one is
creator
omnipresent
omniscient
4. First cause, if it exists, is yet unknown to human beings, and whatever it may be, it is governed by God.
5. The number of laws that together constitute God is not infinite or limitless.
6. Only space is limitless or boundless. Its only content, the universe, is governed by God.
7. Though God cannot be termed all-good, it can be termed good in the sense that it is beneficial, because it brings order and predictability everywhere in the universe.
8. A person can be all-loving, kind, just, and even all-good but only at the discretion of God, which governs everyone, all his works and actions, and even his nature and character.
9. The attributes of God are unity, truth, omnipotence, supremacy, sovereignty, predestination, eternity, immutability, abstractness, spontaneity, aloofness, and self-sufficiency.
10. The attributes absurd to ascribe to God are creativity, infinity, omnipresence, omniscience, incomprehensibility, generosity, wisdom, goodness, love, kindness, justice, and sincerity.

15

GOD AND RELIGION

Neither love nor hatred,
neither pleasure nor pain,
neither virtue nor sin,
neither life nor death—
there is
mechanical movement,
metallic coldness,
echoing silence,
fearful aloofness
in the realm of God.

IT IS RELIGION THAT HAS BEEN USING AS WELL AS PROPAGATING THE IDEA of God, and this is why it is religion itself that has been the source of and that harbours most of the things that have been said about it. So the search for truth in whatever has been said and written about God is for all practical purposes a search for truth in what religion says about it. Thus, in the process of the segregation of the truth from whatever has been said and written about God, after knowing the epithets that correctly describe it and thus the attributes that are possessed by it, now let us focus attention to what religion says about it.

Religion is a system of beliefs and practices that are based on those beliefs. Religious beliefs can be categorised in various ways, one of which can be based on whether they are related to the theoretical or to the practical aspect of religion. The beliefs that are related to the theoretical aspect form the foundation of any religion, and they provide the living sap to the beliefs that are related to its practical aspect. Thus, they can also be termed primary and secondary beliefs. Religion has a vast spread of beliefs. For being concise in the scanning of truth, instead of taking all possible religious beliefs about God, I shall take only the nuclear primary and secondary ones, that is, the very basic beliefs related to the theoretical and practical aspects of religion, the former in the first two sections and the latter in the third one.

KEY RELIGIOUS BOOKS AND SO-CALLED REPRESENTATIVES OF GOD

One of the most elementary beliefs of most religions is that their propagators are messengers or representatives of God, appointed by it especially for conveying its messages, orders, and will to people, which are collected in their key religious books. Can this be correct?

God is the set of all the laws of nature. So it is absurd saying that anyone can be (was, is, or will be) its representative or incarnation; that anyone can see it, hear it, or talk to it; or that any of our religious books was dictated by it. No human being can be God or its representative. None of our religious books was dictated by it or contains its orders, words, will, or message.

In Chapter 11, 'Reasons for the claim', I have already explained why some persons used to claim that they were God's representative or its incarnation. Our religious books were written or dictated by some of these persons with serious intentions of welfare of people. Many of the things contained in these books are relevant for people even in this age—for example, they are living souls of ethics. But before anything is followed from them, it should be checked on the touchstone of reason.

HOW CORRECT ARE THE NUBS OF WHAT EIGHT MAJOR THEISTIC RELIGIONS SAY ABOUT GOD?

In Chapter 9, I placed before you the nuclei of what eight major theistic religions of the world say about God. Now in the light of the knowledge of God and its attributes, let us see that in their description of God, how much is true.

Judaism

God (YHWH: I am that I am, I will be what I will be) is one and only; unique; true; almighty, mighty; universally and eternally sovereign, one who governs; lord, king; sovereign lord over nations of the world and all the earth; sovereign lord over nature, orders the times and seasons; supreme being, highest; eternal, everlasting; universal God, God of all nations, free from territorial restraints; responsible for both good and evil.

Lord of history

God is continuously, immediately, and intimately present and active within the realm of human history, life, events, and actions; he is responsible for whatever political and military successes people obtain.

Continuous activity in the world

Ever present, the present one, responsible for everything: His activity is not only in the past but ongoing and continuous. He continuously, each day, renews the creation and remains actively present in it. He directly and actively participates in the events of the world and human life.

God's will prevails

Except human actions, everything happens according to God. (This is partially correct. Fully correct is 'God is responsible for whatever happens without exception.')

Christianity

God (YHWH (pronounced Yahweh): I am that I am, I will be what I will be) is one, sole; unique; almighty, omnipotent, powerful, mighty; has the absolute power, of great might; overwhelming, immutable, ultimately prevailing; greatest; sovereign, God has everlasting sovereignty; lord, ruler, king; universal; king over heaven and all the earth, God of all of the earth, God of the nations; lord of world history; eternal; self-sufficient.

Continuous activity in the world

Ever present, the present one: His activity is not only in the past but ongoing and continuous. He continuously, each day, renews the creation.

God's will prevails

Except human actions, everything happens according to God. (This is partially correct. Fully correct is 'God is responsible for whatever happens without exception.')

Governs nature

He orders the times and seasons.

Lord of history

God is continuously, immediately, and intimately present and active within the realm of human history, life, events, and actions.

ISLAM

God (Allah) is one and only; unique; supreme being, unparalleled, exalted, highest; without any partner; great, source of all greatness; sovereign; lord of everyone, lord of the worlds, master of everyone, everyone and everything obeys him; independent; self-sufficient; reigns unchallenged on the whole kingdom of heaven and earth; the unshaken; the truth, real, the real truth, the true one; eternal, unborn, uncreated, beyond time, the first being.

Unchanging

The way in which God deals does not change with time.

Almighty

Omnipotent, all-powerful, immaculately powerful; mighty, possesses might: He governs everything that exists all by himself, without any partner. In the universe, including in the life of human beings, nothing happens or nothing is performed unless it is by the will of Allah. Thus, human beings are subservient to the divine, or God's role in relation to humans is that of a commander.

Architect of destiny

God determines the destiny of people.

Without relatives

God has no relatives—he does not have a wife, sons, or daughters.

TAOISM

God (Tao) is one; spontaneous; supreme master, ruler of the universe; primordial, uncreated, beyond change, permanent.

Unity in diversity

In all the pulsations, multiplicity, cyclic processes, and periodical mutations and transformations, that is, in all the reversions that take place in the universe between yin and yang (see chapter 9, 'Taoism', 'Yin and yang'), the underlying undifferentiated, primordial, unchanging unity, the permanent Tao, is never lost.

Continuous creation

Tao shapes the universe continuously out of primordial chaos and simultaneously keeps on transforming it by the alternations of yin and yang. (This is correct only in the sense that Tao directs the shaping and transformation of the universe, not that it plays a physical role.) The two phases of creation, the shaping of all beings and their transformation through the alternations of yin and yang, are not only simultaneous but also perpetual.

CONFUCIANISM

God [Pinyin TIAN (Heaven), T'ien (Heaven), Ti (Lord), Shang-ti (Supreme Lord)] is almighty, all-powerful; great, greatest; supreme being; supreme lord, lord on high, ruler, supreme ruler; grand; law or principle; master of life and death; fate; active; vast; abstract; impersonal, aloof.

Heaven's will is supreme

The will of Heaven is supreme and infallible.

The way of Heaven

Heaven's behaviour is based on constant principles.

Decides events

Heaven determines the actions of all beings and wealth, dignity, honour, and appointments of humans.

Predetermines events

Heaven predetermines life and death, riches and honour.

Giver

The nature, supreme virtue, and good conscience are conferred on beings by Heaven. Heaven shapes the nature of humans and bestows on them the virtues, such as nobility, humanity, excellence, conscience, benevolence, and sagehood.

ZOROASTRIANISM

God [Ormazd, Ahura Mazda (Wise Lord)] is one; omnipotent; greatest, supreme, having no parallel; lord, one who governs; eternal, immortal; true.

HINDUISM

God (Om, Om Tut Sut, Bruhm)[1] is one; absolute; unique; lord; supreme lord of all beings, the universe; king, ruler, master; one who controls everyone and everything; the supreme being; the greatest; eternal, unborn, primal, ancient, imperishable; unchanging; immovable; truth; the object of knowledge; not known to anyone in complete.

Almighty

Everything is like a puppet in the hands of or like an instrument in the control of the divine.

One who gives the results of deeds

God decides the results of the work people do.

Decides the destiny

God predestines events.

Unattached

He is indifferent and unattached to everything, including good and evil, virtue and sin, love and hatred, and all the deeds and their fruits.

Impartial

No one is unlovable or dear to him, whether he is good or bad, virtuous or sinful, pious or impious.

SIKHISM

God [Sut-Kurtar (True Creator), Sut-Nam (True Name), Wah-Guru (Hail Guru), whose symbol is *om* and *ik-om-kar* (one-*om*-creator)][2] is one; unique; the truth, true, true forever; God abides in the realm of truth; supreme being; great, greatest of all; unrivalled; eternal, primal, uncreated, immortal, imperishable, ever present; formless.

Almighty

Everything that happens in the universe, including in the life of any person, is according to the will, command, or pleasure of God. All the powers have their source in him.

Sovereign

Master; lord, supreme lord, lord of the world; king, the king of kings: He is not subordinate to anyone; he is independent. He is the supreme master of all.

Decides the destiny

Architect of destiny: nothing happens in the universe, including in the life of human beings, except what is preordained by God.

Beyond change

He never changes; through all time, he remains the same.

This is the extent to which the nubs of what eight major theistic religions of the world say about God, given in Chapter 9, are correct. Now I leave it up to you

1. to place the religions in ascending or descending order depending on the degree of the correctness of their themes about God and
2. to find out the causes of a particular place of any particular religion in that hierarchy.

TRUTH OF RELIGIOUS ETHICS AND CODES OF CONDUCTS

A large part of what religions say is stuffed with the instructions for the ways of realisation of God, that is, what people should do and what they should not to achieve God, to know it, or to communicate with it. The beliefs that support this practical aspect of religion can be termed secondary beliefs if those related to the theoretical aspect are termed primary beliefs because the former have their roots in the latter. In the last two sections, you saw the truth behind the nuclear beliefs associated to the theoretical aspect of religion. In this section let me show you the truth behind some nuclear beliefs related to the practical aspects of religion.

Desire

Desire means wish or want. In almost every religion, desire is seen as a hurdle in the way of salvation and realisation of God. This is why the more a person is seen as desireless, the more he is considered closer to God—priests and mystics of every religion try to follow the code of desirelessness and they are considered closer to God than others are. In the eastern religions such as Taoism, Confucianism, Hinduism, and Sikhism, mostly because they are mystical in essence, for salvation as well as realisation of God, the code of desirelessness is given much more emphasis than it is given in other religions, and forming a part of their central theme, it is preached not only to the priests and mystics but to everyone. In whichever religion to whatever extent there be the emphasis on the concept of desirelessness for the realisation of God, the reasons are almost the same.

In most religions, meditation on God and its virtues is seen as a primary way for its realisation. Desire is a major hurdle in the path of meditation. On one hand, during meditation, it distracts the mind of a person from her object of meditation, on the other hand it reduces the time of meditation by involving her in other works for its fulfilment. Thus, it works in twofold ways to keep a person away from proper meditation. This is as true for meditation on God as it is for meditation on any other thing. Thus, a reason that desire is looked down upon by religions is that it is a hurdle in the way of meditation on God, which is considered a primary way to realise it.

God was believed to be almighty and supreme being, the greatest possible being. Philosophers assumed that a person who realises God acquires a state of perpetual bliss, that is, he becomes beyond all types of what they thought as instabilities and flaws, such as happiness, sadness, anger, excitement, and fear, and always remains in a state of unwavering calmness or peace. They further thought that when a person, by his own efforts, reaches this state of perpetual calmness—becomes free from so-called flaws, such as, happiness, sadness, excitement, anger, and fear—he gets its grace in the form of its realisation. Desire, affection, ego, pain, pleasure, and so on are basically the main factors that cause happiness, sadness, excitement, anger, fear, and so on and disturb the mental peace of a person. Since achievement of a perpetual calm state of mind was thought to be a means for realisation of God and since desire is one of the main and basic factors that perturb the calmness of mind, desirelessness was preached as an important desirable attribute in a person aspiring to the realisation of God. This is the second reason religion condemns desire.

Many philosophers who were indifferent to the existence of God and its realisation thought that the state of continuous mental calmness or peace was the greatest thing that a person could achieve, and since they saw desire as a basic factor that disturbed it, they preached desirelessness. But only few people were interested in achieving perpetual mental peace. Most people were interested in the realisation of God. Therefore, to benefit maximum number of people by their idea of desirelessness for mental peace, they preached desirelessness as a means to realise God.

In short, the propagators of religions and the philosophers preached desirelessness because they saw desire as a hurdle in the meditation on God and in attaining peace of mind, which they thought to be as well as projected as means for its realisation.

Before anything can be said on the relation between desirelessness and realisation of God, the viability of desirelessness should itself be put to a test.

Since we are living as well as active beings, we have needs, which give birth to desires. Most of our desires, in some or other way, take birth from our needs. Desires work as compelling forces for us to put efforts for the fulfilment of our needs, which in turn is necessary for the continuation of our life and progress. It means that we have desires because we live and we live because we have desires, or desires are inevitable as well as essential for our lives.

It is not that we always have desires. Although most of our activities need the fuel of desires from the beginning to the end, there can of course be but a few moments of desirelessness during them. This stands true for both physical and mental activities. Longer timespans of desirelessness are possible but exclusively in inactive states such as deep sleep and unconsciousness.

To live you need to perform useful and productive activities, which need to be fuelled by your desires; since you cannot remain inactive for too long, you cannot always be in a desireless state, and if you have to have desires, it does not matter from the religious point of view whether they are intense or slight, big or small, numerous or only one: the desire to be desireless. However selfless and benevolent it may seem, the desire of Buddh[3] to see everyone without desire and woe was as much a desire as that of a king for more territory, that of a scholar for more knowledge, or that of a businessperson for more money. Since you cannot be altogether free from desires, the demand of any religion for your being completely desireless is irrational from the very outset, or in whatever religion wherever there is a concept of permanent complete desirelessness, it is wrong and deceptive. Since our activities are generated as well as fuelled by our desires, we are least desireless when we are active; therefore, the concept of desireless or selfless work is even more absurd and deceptive. The concepts of complete desirelessness and desireless works are absurd, so the question whether desirelessness can be helpful in realisation of God is also absurd.

What is true for desire is true for all other feelings, such as happiness, sadness, anger, excitement, fear, and affection: their existence in human beings, to proper extent, is as essential and as inevitable for their lives as that of desire is. How will a person work hard if she does not feel happy with her success or sad due to her failure? how will she resist atrocities if they do not make her angry? how will she care for the elderly and the young ones if she does not feel affectionate towards them? and how will humanity exist if human beings do not work, not continuously fight against atrocities and transgression of their rights, and not care for the elderly and the young ones? Thus, the concept of any person becoming absolutely free from them is as absurd as the concept of absolute desirelessness.

In the same way as there are moments when one is desireless, there are respective moments and timespans of her being free from other feelings too. There are also timespans when one remains in the state of absolute mental peace, but such state occurs momentarily or for short timespans when she is active; the longer timespans can occur only when she is both physically and mentally inactive such as in deep sleep and unconsciousness; and since a person needs to remain active to keep on living, she cannot always be in the state of absolute mental peace. Thus, the concept that a person can realise God by achieving the state of perpetual mental calmness is also absurd.

Here I should remind you that the propagators of religions and the philosophers preached desirelessness because they saw desire as a hurdle in meditation on God and in attaining peace of mind, which they thought as well as projected to be means for its realisation. Now that we know that complete freedom from desires and other such feelings is not possible and as impossible is the achievement of perpetual calm state of mind and thus the question whether God can be realised by complete desirelessness or perpetual calmness of mind is absurd, it is worth looking into whether timespans of calmness of mind, such as those achieved during work, meditation, and deep sleep, can help in realisation of God or not.

God is the set of all the laws of nature. Thus, to realise God what you can do is to know it and its attributes, and it is absurd to say that you can realise it by achieving the state of perfect mental peace for whatever length of timespan.

The wrong idea that a person can realise God by achieving the state of perpetual absolute mental calmness took birth from the perception that one who has realised God achieves such mental state. Now that you know God, will you achieve the state of perpetual perfect mental calmness or peace? As I have repeatedly said, the feelings such as desire, fear, happiness, sadness, anger, and excitement, to proper extents, are essential for your life. Since they are synonymous to disturbances in mental calmness, although you can have moments of calmness when you are active and long timespans of calmness when you are inactive, you cannot always be in the state of absolute mental peace. But the knowledge that you have achieved as a result of the realisation of God—the knowledge that whatever happens in the universe, including in your or anyone's life, is predetermined by God—will certainly make a difference. It is similar to the difference that I have already mentioned in Chapter 7 (Destiny and You) while discussing the effect of the knowledge of the theorem of destiny on human life: The knowledge that God predestines every event that takes place will calm you when you will be in grief, anger, worry, tension, and so on, telling you that it is God, not you, who is ultimately responsible for whatever happens, initially making you free from extreme ends, that is, from the feelings of extreme worry, tension, anger, sorrow, and so on. This difference, which this knowledge will make in terms of your mental peace, will go on increasing as time passes by, as it, the knowledge, goes deeper and deeper into your heart through your brain.

Prayer

In reference to God, prayer means a request or petition to it. The desires expressed during the prayers before God are the desires people have, such as of material goods, success, victory, peace, salvation, and sanctity.

There was a time when a human being knew very little about nature. His life depended largely on the mercy of nature, on which he had a very little control. Since God was believed to exercise authority over it, he had no option except to desire it to save him from the wrath of the latter and to be favourable to him. This desire inevitably led to the belief that God is kind and merciful because if it were not so, why would it help anyone, and if it, the almighty, would not help, who else would do so? Thus, God was established among the mobs as kind and merciful. In terms of religion, after the nuclear belief that there exists a great, mysterious power alias God that exercises complete authority over nature, the belief that holds the utmost importance is that God is kind and merciful because it makes the idea of God seemingly useful and alluring for everyone and in this way provides a purpose to religion and helps its existence as well as propagation. The desire of human beings for the help of the almighty is the root of the belief that it is kind and merciful, which in turn is the root of the phenomenon of prayer, that is, putting requests and desires before it with the hope that it will be kind enough to fulfil them.

If you look into yourself, you will find that you have numerous small and big desires. In your prayers you ask God to fulfil your desires, and when I say this, remember that however pious it may seem, a desire is nothing except a desire. Thus, in your prayer when you ask God for world peace, you have no less a desire than when you ask for more profit in your business. Generally, the desires that you ask God to fulfil in your prayers are from among those that you find difficult to execute. But this level of difficulty is different for different persons: the prayer of a person may be so free from the expression of desires that even in her thorny days her prayer may be merely meditation on God, and there are people who do not hesitate to ask in their prayers even for petty things, such as, to send a taxi.

Your prayers in general provide a feeling of peace and satisfaction to you because they give you the hope that God will help you in the fulfilment of your desires by removing the hurdles or that it will at least not create hurdles if you think that you have done something to make it angry. It is this feeling of peace and satisfaction that makes prayer so popular among people, which makes the belief that God is kind and merciful a cornerstone of almost every religion.

Thousands and thousands of people have been dying in volcanic eruptions, earthquakes, floods, landslides, droughts, and so on, which shows that it is absurd to use 'mercy' for nature, and since nature was considered to be governed by God, it was also absurd to term God kind and merciful. This was never very difficult for any unbiased person to observe. Yet God was termed kind and merciful because people needed it to be so or because a merciless God might have been a matter of discussion for philosophers but was of no use for the masses. Most of the propagators of religions who claimed that they were representative, relative, or messenger of God essentially needed to stress that it is kind and merciful to make the concept of God seemingly useful and alluring to people so that it might become possible for them to begin and carry out their mission in its name. The high place that they awarded to prayer in religion by giving birth to the belief that it brings one closer to God and by asserting that it softens its attitude and induces it to fulfil one's desires was to increase the faith and attraction of people in God so as to further facilitate solving their purposes.

As I have already said in Chapter 11, God is a set of laws, and therefore it is absurd to think of closeness or distance with it or to describe it as good, kind, just, loving, or merciful, which would have been clear to you by observing the happenings of the world around you even when you were just believing in God, without knowing it, to be a power that governs nature. Thus, the belief that a prayer can bring the prayer close to God or can please it is also absurd.

Laws of nature are beyond any type of change, and since God is the set of all the laws of nature, it too is beyond any type of change. No matter how much you pray or worship it, you cannot bring about any change in it or its attitude towards you (the way it decides, determines, or governs your life).

Including your prayers, everything in the universe happens (happened in the past, is happening at present, and will happen in the future) according to God. The future of the universe, which of course includes the future of every one of us, is predetermined and unchangeable, and God, which predetermines it, is itself unchangeable. God decides the destiny of the universe, and since your prayers directed to it cannot at all affect or change it, they cannot change the destiny of the universe, including that of anyone or anything in it, by even a single bit.

Thus, since God is an abstract and unchangeable set of laws, it is no use praying to it. It is absurd even to think that it hears your prayers. Prayers used to fill you with peace and satisfaction because you believed that the almighty God listens to them and helps you in the fulfilment of the desires you express in them. Now, when you know that it is absurd to think that your prayer is heard by God, changes its attitude towards you, changes your future, or helps you in any way, you may stop praying to God, and in any case if you decide to continue with them, they may not give you as much satisfaction as they used to give before by providing the hope of fulfilment of desires or they may become free from the expression of desires to be transformed into utter meditation.

Sinful and virtuous deeds

Morals are necessary for good or welfare of people and smooth running of any society. Mostly, morals have been subject of religions; they are full of moral codes of conducts, invented by their propagators in their efforts of welfare of people.

Sin is defined as transgression of religious morals. Thus, a sinful deed is one that violates the religious morals. On the other hand, a virtuous deed is one that is in accordance with religious morals.

In any religion since the giving of moral codes of conducts is aimed at welfare of people, the categorisation of immoral and moral deeds as sinful and virtuous respectively is also the same: the good or welfare of people. But not everyone was intelligent enough to understand this, and people could leave the path of virtue and commit sin for their lasting or momentary profit against the interest of the society and against their own long-term good due to lack of farsightedness. In other words, just giving moral codes of conducts, categorising deeds as virtuous and sinful, and telling that the path of virtue is for good and that of sin is against the interest of everyone was not enough to make a person perform virtuous deeds or to stop her from committing sin.

How to induce people on the path of virtue and to make them fear from committing sin or working against the good of the society was a major problem faced by persons who laid down codes of conducts and categorised deeds as virtuous and sinful for them with the aim of their welfare. In an effort to solve this problem, they mentioned that virtuous deeds result in health, happiness, prosperity, fame, and so on, and sinful deeds result in the opposite, that is, diseases, poverty, disrepute, and so on. Somewhat as it is today, it has never been an uncommon sight that many virtuous people have to face numerous types of difficulties, whereas many sinners enjoy easy, healthy, luxurious, and progressive life. People could see that there was no direct connection between virtuous and sinful deeds and their mentioned results. Thus, it was necessary to relate virtuous and sinful deeds with unidentified things such as soul, afterlife, and God, and it was added that virtuous deeds result in God's favour, closeness with it, and a place in heaven after death and sinful deeds result in God's wrath, increase in distance with it, and torturous afterlife, and so on. This is how the propagators of religions gave birth to the belief that sinful deeds result in diseases, poverty, disrepute, torture in afterlife, wrath of God, increase in distance with it, and so on, although they themselves did not know God; were not sure about afterlife; and knew that there is no direct connection between sinful deeds and such factors as economic condition, health, and reputation. Virtuous deeds were described in an opposite way, as if sinful and virtuous deeds were like acid and base, counteracting each other's effect.

As time passed by, the number of deeds categorised as sinful or virtuous and the number and types of punishments and rewards mentioned respectively for sinful and virtuous deeds went on increasing, and because of the multiplicity of definitions, the situation has become so complex that you can categorise almost every deed as sinful or virtuous and your life may become one of perpetual tension and actual hell if you sincerely try to follow the so-called right path or voice of your conscience. If you find it difficult to believe, read a book that tells about all the religious morals and try to follow it sincerely or try to always obey the voice of your conscience. Also with the passage of time, the clutches of these false theories of virtue and sin went on tightening on the hearts and brains of people and it went on becoming more and more difficult for anyone to trace that the real aim of defining virtue and sin and categorising deeds as virtuous and sinful is the good or welfare of persons and to maintain order, peace, and harmony in the societies or civilisations. The right path is illuminated not only by faith, morals, and conscience but also by reason, constitution, and discretion.

God is the set of all the laws of nature. Everything in the universe happens according to God. All the actions and deeds of a person are a part of whatever occurs in the universe, and since everything happens according to God, everything that a person does, whether it is sinful or virtuous, is done under the direction of God. God predestines all your sinful and virtuous deeds. Because of your sinful or virtuous deeds, if you bring upon yourself or people any harm or profit, that too is predestined by God.

Since God is a set of laws, it is absurd to think that your sinful deeds make it angry or take you away from it or your virtuous deeds make it happy or bring you closer to it. On the contrary, as I showed above, whatever you do, whether virtuous or sinful, is perfectly according to God. The deliverance of this sacred knowledge may prove to be dangerous if it is not supplemented by the fact that in general—and this is a general fact, not an exact scientific one as the former—those whom God blesses with virtuous deeds are also blessed with glory and those whom it curses with sinful deeds are also cursed with notoriety, disdain, and fear. Since everything happens according to God, the reward that a person receives in the form of recognition and respect is organised by God, for the meritorious deed that he does in its direction, and the punishment that he receives in the form of fine, imprisonment, execution, and so on, is also organised by God, for the crime that he does in its direction, according to its discretion.

This was a brief insight into just three of the innumerable codes of conducts given by religion as means of realisation of God. As illustrated in the above three cases, besides the displayed purpose, the realisation of God, they have been fabricated to solve various other purposes, related to almost every aspect of individual and social life, such as order and peace in the society; welfare of the oppressed, the weak, and the aged; physical and mental health of people; and facilitation of the growth and propagation of religion. Since God is the set of all the laws of nature, however sincerely one follows the religious codes of conducts, she cannot realise God just by that. The only way to realise God is to know and understand it and its attributes.

Now that God has been revealed, the theistic religions have been deprived of the main portion of their central theme. In this situation how much relevance is religion left with?

REMAINING RELEVANCE OF RELIGION

Religion is a system of beliefs and practices based on those beliefs. These beliefs and practices are deeply associated with curiosities, desires, fears, and concerns of people, such as curiosities about nature, life, and existence; desires for power, longevity, material, knowledge, and peace; and fears of death, conflict, disrepute, and dearth. It is not that people do not put efforts for their desirables, but they do not want to leave any stone unturned by taking any chance with whatever is hidden in the unknown, though the same hidden becomes the quest of life for some persons. God forms the central theme of most religions. The reason for the belief in God and for worshipping it is also the same: the curiosity about the unknown and the hidden, the hope of fulfilment of desires, and the influence of fears.

Science has a vast spread, yet it has limits. Where the realm of science ends, that of religion, the system of beliefs and practices based on those beliefs, begins. As science grows, it takes away more and more land ruled over by religion, and this is why religion goes on weakening day after day. It is only because of the development in the field of science that we have come to know God, which obviously is another blow, a big blow, to religion. The realm of science can be compared to the areas lit in a moonless dark night; the rest of the areas covered with mist and darkness symbolise the realm of religion. As we go on putting up more and more lights of scientific knowledge, the area under the cover of darkness of ignorance that symbolises the realm of religion goes on decreasing, but since we are unaware of the total area covered by the darkness and mistiness of ignorance, we cannot say when we will be able to occupy it completely, when there will be no place for religion to reside in, or when religion will be simply extinct.

God is the pivot of the theistic religions. While revealing God and segregating the truth about it from important religious beliefs, I showed that

1. Most of the religious codes of conducts are aimed at the benefit of personal and social life, and it is absurd to think that God can be realised by following them:
   (a) Desire and other feelings, in balanced proportions, are essential for our existence and progress, and it is absurd to think that God can be realised by their removal or even that they can be removed totally.
   (b) It is absurd to think that prayer or worship will make God happy, will make it easy for a person to get her desirables, or will change her destiny.
   (c) The basic aim of categorising deeds as virtuous and sinful is the general good or welfare of people, and the realisation of God by someone is independent of how sinful or virtuous she is.
2. The only way to realise God is to know it and its attributes.
3. God is the set of all the laws that take part in governing the phenomena, events, or happenings that take place in the universe: the set of all the laws of nature.
4. Everything that happens in the universe, including everything that happens in one's life and everything one does, happens according to God—is predetermined or predestined by God.

Now, when we know all this, what is the relevance of religion for us?

Even after the revelation of God and the proof of the theorem of destiny, much remains in the realm of ignorance as a subject for religion. For example, the topics of soul, afterlife, reincarnation, different levels of existence, *sumadhi*[4] (the supreme state that can be acquired by a person according to yoag[5]), ecstasy, salvation, and many other paranormal, mystic, and extrasensory phenomena that are still beyond the reach of science will continue to attract and interest people and therefore, will continue to be addressed by religion and exploited by its authorities and agents.

Culture of a person depends on the geography of her native land and the history of her ancestors. Culture is older than religion is, but over the years religion has become closely associated with culture—so closely that our cultural identity is generally determined by our religious identity, not by the place of our residence or by our origin. The reverence or worship of God has become deeply embedded into our cultural practices. Thus, what previously were cultural practices of a particular area have become known as practices of the religion that originated in that area, and when that religion spreads to other parts of the world, these practices also spread to these parts, even if they may be irrelevant for the people living there due to the difference in their geographical situation. After the revelation of God, being devoid of its faith and reverence, the religious practices will become closer to reason, aptness, geography, culture, and celebration.

Numerous subjects being unaffected by the knowledge of God, of its might, and of the reach of destiny, will continue to remain in the realm of religion. One of them is morality, which has unquestioned significance for the benefit of people; since it is beyond science as well as constitution, it will continue to be a subject of, to take its living sap from, or to have its roots in religion.

Thus, even after being deprived of its central theme, God, religion will remain relevant for us to a substantial extent, more in the form of culture than in the form of faith.

Part 4
Summary

16

GOD IS ALMIGHTY

A straw in the stream,
a cloud in the sky,
a character in a play—
what am I?
Just a puppet in its hands.

GOD IS THE SET OF ALL THE LAWS THAT TAKE PART IN GOVERNING THE phenomena, events, or happenings that take place in the universe, that is, the set of all the laws of nature. In the universe everything happens according to it, or every phenomenon, event, or happening that takes place in the universe is determined, decided, designed, directed, organised, or governed by God. Therefore, it is one who governs nature or is the ruler of the universe, rightly termed almighty, omnipotent, and supreme being.

All that happens (happened in the past, is happening at present, and will happen in the future) in the universe lies in the ambit of destiny—is predestined as well as inevitable or unchangeable. This predestined and unchangeable course of events or the destiny of the universe, including destiny of not only you but everyone and everything in it, is determined or decided by God: God is one who decides destiny or is the master of destiny.

Whatever has to occur in your life in future, even including your future thoughts, dreams, and feelings, is predetermined and unchangeable. It is God that predestines your future.

Every bit of you and your life is decided by God. Your nature, personality, capabilities, weaknesses, achievements, and failures and even your imaginations, decisions, feelings, and so on are all determined or decided by God—it decides not only your successes and failures but also your post-success vainglory and post-failure sadness.

It torments you with a failure, even if you work according to its directions. It awards you with the fruits of successes on the paths that it itself makes you travel. It punishes you for the crimes for which it itself is responsible. It blesses you with applauses for the virtuous deeds it destines for you.

A straw in the stream,
a cloud in the sky,
a character in a play—
what are you?
Just a puppet in its hands.

Appendices

Part A
The Scientific Proof

A

INTRODUCTION

A STATEMENT OR THEOREM CANNOT BE UNIVERSALLY ACCEPTABLE AS truth unless it is proved scientifically. This is why I have also proved the theorem of destiny scientifically and presented the proof here, in Appendix B.

Objections can be raised on the proof of the theorem of destiny on the basis of the principle of indeterminacy. I have given the explanation to these objections in Appendix C.

There is an ultimate limit to the accuracy with which the future can be predicted. The reason of this has been given in Appendix D.

Something that is predestined cannot be changeable or avoidable, or what is predestined has to be unchangeable or inevitable. It means that it is unnecessary to use 'unchangeable' or 'inevitable' for something that is characterised as predestined. Till now I have been using 'unchangeable' or 'inevitable' along with 'predestined' for 'future' in the statement of the theorem of destiny because I wanted to emphasise the unchangeability or inevitability of the future, but now since the scientific analysis is about to begin, it is necessary to be precise as well as concise, to state the theorem of destiny for this part as

The future is predestined.

B

SCIENTIFIC PROOF OF THE THEOREM OF DESTINY

The future is just a projection of the past.

THE PROOF OF THE THEOREM OF DESTINY PRESENTED HERE IS BASICALLY similar to those presented in Chapters 4 and 5—closer to that in Chapter 5, in fact. One of the main differences is that instead of using the principle of consecutive frames [(4.5), (5.5), or (5.6)] as the starting point, the proof here uses *principle of experiment*, which I have derived from the fundamental nature of experiments.

The proof is scientific in the sense that I have tried to make it flawless from the point of view of physics, for example, everything has been viewed relative to reference frames. To be understood, it requires intermediate-level knowledge of physics.

B.1 THE THEOREM OF DESTINY

The statement of the theorem of destiny, after being modified in appendix A, is given as

The future is predestined. ... (B.1)

B.2 PARTINO

The universe is constituted by matter and energy.

Let

1. the constituent of the universe (matter and/or energy) be denoted by *mave* (**ma**tter + wa**ve**)
2. a minute portion of mave or a tiny building block of the universe such as a photon, quark, proton, neutron, or electron be denoted by *parton* (**par**ticle + pho**ton**)
3. the smallest possible amount of mave or the most elementary building block of the universe, such as a photon, quark, or lepton, be denoted by *partino*

... (B.2)

The assumption (B.2-3) implies that the universe, at the most elementary level, is constituted by partinos only. Thus,

> At any instant relative to a reference frame, a corporeal thing is either a partino or a group of partinos at the most elementary level. ... (B.3)

and

> At any instant relative to a reference frame, the universe is basically a group of partinos. ... (B.4)

B.3 IDENTITY

For the appendix, *identity* is defined as follows:

> At any instant relative to a reference frame, the identity of something is the set of all its properties, attributes, qualities, or characteristics or is its complete or 100 per cent description. ... (B.5)

Further,

> At any instant relative to a reference frame, a physical property or characteristic of a partino can be represented by an equation containing its name, numerical value, and unit. For example, at any instant relative to a reference frame, the velocity of a partino may be given as

$$\text{velocity} = (6i + 8j + 10k) \times 10^7 \text{ m/sec}$$

... (B.6)

From (B.5) and (B.6), it follows that

> At any instant relative to a reference frame, the identity of a partino can be represented by the set of all the equations giving the values of respectively all the physical quantities describing it, such as of its mass, location, velocity, frequency, and charge. ... (B.7)

Keeping in view the definition of identity (B.5),

> At any instant relative to a reference frame, the identity of a group of partinos is the set of identities of all the partinos constituting the group. ... (B.8)

Thus,

> At any instant relative to a reference frame, the identity of a group of partinos can be represented by the set that contains all the sets that respectively represent [may be according to (B.7)] the identities of all the partinos constituting the group.

From (B.3) and (B.8), it follows that

> At any instant relative to a reference frame, the identity of any corporeal thing is the set of identities of all the partinos constituting it. ... (B.9)

It follows from (B.8) and (B.4) that

> At any instant relative to a reference frame, the identity of the universe is the set of identities of all the partinos constituting it. ... (B.10)

Thus,

> At any instant relative to a reference frame, the identity of the universe can be represented by the set that contains all the sets that respectively represent [may be according to (B.7)] the identities of all the partinos that constitute it.

B.4 REPRESENTATION OF HAPPENINGS IN TERMS OF IDENTITY

Let

1. an infinitely large space be denoted by *V*
2. the total content of V be denoted by *G*
3. a reference frame be denoted by *R*
4. an instant and a timespan relative to R be denoted by *t* and *T* respectively

... (B.11)

At *t* relative to R, the identity of G is complete as well as exact description of G; phenomena, events, or happenings exhibited by G; or whatever happens, occurs, or takes place inside V. Thus,

> Relative to R, the ordered set that contains all the identities acquired by G at respectively all the instants of *T* in the sequence they (the instants or the identities) occur [the ordered set that contains the identity acquired by G at each instant of *T* in the sequence it (the instant or the identity) occurs] completely as well as exactly represents all the phenomena exhibited by G or whatever occurs inside V during *T*. ... (B.12)

As you know,

> The universe is the total content of an infinitely large space. ... (B.13)

Keeping in view (B.11-1) and (B.11-2), it follows from (B.13) that

> The universe lies in the category of G. ... (B.14)

It follows from (B.14) that (B.12), which has been stated for G, stands true for the universe too:

> Relative to a reference frame R, the ordered set that contains all the identities acquired by the universe at respectively all the instants of a timespan *T* in the sequence they (the instants or the identities) occur [the ordered set that contains the identity acquired by the universe at each instant of *T* in the sequence it (the instant or the identity) occurs] completely as well as exactly represents all the phenomena exhibited by the universe

> or whatever happens in the universe during that timespan, *T*. ... (B.15)

B.5 TRANSFERABLE REFERENCE FRAME

> No partino is eternal, or every partino exists for a limited timespan. ... (B.16)

Moreover,

> A group of partinos exists till all the members of the group exist simultaneously. ... (B.17)

Keeping in view (B.16), it follows from (B.17) that

> No group of partinos is eternal, or every group of partinos exists for a limited timespan. ... (B.18)

A reference frame can only be defined with respect to a corporeal thing, and since a corporeal thing is either a partino or a group of partinos at the most elementary level (B.3), a reference frame can primarily be defined with respect to either a partino or a group of partinos. Thus, a reference frame exists till the partino or the group of partinos with respect to which it is defined exists. Since every partino and every group of partinos exists for a limited timespan [(B.16) and (B.18)], a reference frame defined with respect to any partino or any group of partinos exists for a limited timespan, or since no partino and no group of partinos is eternal, no reference frame defined with respect to any partino or any group of partinos is eternal.

For the proof of the theorem of destiny, there is need of a reference frame whose life span is longer than is the life span of the partino or the group of partinos with respect to which it is defined. This need is fulfilled by a *transferable reference frame* (TRF). What I term

> A transferable reference frame (TRF) is a reference frame that is defined with respect to a series of partinos and/or groups of partinos in such a way that at a definite instant, which may be termed a *transfer instant*, before a partino or a group of partinos with respect to which it is defined ceases to exist, it is transferred to, associated with, or defined with respect to any other partino or any other group of partinos. ... (B.19)

So

1. At any instant a TRF is defined with respect to only one partino or only one group of partinos.
2. Its two consecutive carriers coexist for at least one instant: the transfer instant.
3. Its first carrier takes it from its birth instant to the instant that immediately precedes its first transfer instant; the last carrier, from the last transfer instant to the last instant of its life; any other carrier, from a transfer instant to the instant that immediately precedes the next transfer instant.
4. It follows a continuous course in time, and it exists till it is continued to be transferred to, associated with, or defined with respect to new partinos and/or new groups of partinos or till new partinos and/or new groups of partinos that can carry it according to the criteria mentioned in its definition continue to be available.
5. A TRF is fundamentally a continuous series of reference frames that are set end to end in time—the lives of two consecutive members of this series do not have any gap of time between themselves, nor do they overlap each other for any time.

The above definition (B.19) also implies that

> A reference frame defined with respect to one partino or one group of partinos is a TRF having only one carrier or is the simplest type of TRF and therefore, being just a special case of TRF, lies in its category.

A TRF defined in such a way that after coming into existence, it exists forever can be termed an *eternal transferable reference frame* (ETRF).

A TRF can be of the type that is defined with respect to new partinos and/or new groups of partinos as time passes by; it can also be of the type whose definition is complete when it begins its life or before the second instant of its life. Let the latter type of TRF be termed *predefined transferable reference frame* (PTRF). Thus,

> A predefined transferable reference frame (PTRF) is a type of TRF that is defined once for all at its birth instant or whose definition is complete before the second instant of its life.

The definition of a PTRF, being complete when it begins its life or before the second instant of its life, contains

1. (a) the identification of its first carrier and birth instant.
   (b) the way in which it is defined with respect to its first carrier.
2. a set of rules that from time to time (as time passes by after its birth) governs
   (a) the selection of its transfer instants and its other (other than the first one) carriers
   (b) the decision of ways in which it is defined with respect to its other carriers

Thus, among all the partinos and/or groups of partinos that carry it one by one in a series, the first one is that which is selected for the purpose and the way in which it is defined with respect to the first carrier is that which is decided for it beforehand (before the second instant of its life) and mentioned in its definition; the selection of its other carriers and the decision of the ways in which it gets defined with respect to them respectively is done automatically with the passage of time after its birth according to the set of rules that too is decided for it beforehand and mentioned in its definition. This shows the relevance of 'predefined' in its name, predefined transferable reference frame.

Being a type of TRF, a PTRF too exists till any partino or any group of partinos that is eligible to carry it according to the conditions mentioned in its definition is available. A PTRF defined in such a way that after coming into existence, it exists for ever can be termed an *eternal predefined transferable reference frame* (EPTRF). For example,

Example B.1

A type of EPTRF, which may be denoted by R_e, is defined with respect to the partinos of the universe as follows:

1. At any instant it is defined with respect to or carried by only one partino, and throughout the time a partino carries it, its origin remains fixed to the centre of mass of and it remains stationary with respect to that partino.
2. Among all the partinos that carry it one by one in a series, the first one is that which is selected for the purpose, to carry it starting from a selected birth instant, and the identity it has relative to this partino is also what is decided for it.
3. The selection of its transfer instants and its other carrier partinos (other than the first one) and the decision of its identities relative to them respectively is done automatically as time passes by after

> its birth with the help of this rule: At the last instant of existence of any of its carrier partinos or just before a partino that carries it ceases to exist, it is transferred to, associated with, or defined with respect to another partino of the universe that at that instant lies closest to its origin in such a way that the directions of its axes on the new partino at the transfer instant remain exactly the same respectively as they would be if it were not transferred, if it were still held by its previous carrier.

From the above definition of R_e, it is clear that being automatically transferred from one partino to another, it exists till any partino of the universe to which it can be transferred exists. Since the universe is eternal, some or other partino will always be available to which it can be transferred according to the criterion mentioned in its definition, and therefore after taking birth it exists for ever.

B.6 PRINCIPLE OF EXPERIMENT

It is observed that

> Relative to a reference frame, when an experiment is repeatedly performed in a definite way, the sets of totality of observations corresponding to the performances, instead of being the same, are similar to a limited but definite extent.

For example,

Example B.2

Relative to a reference frame fixed in a definite way to a particular plane, horizontal cemented floor on the earth, when a cricket or hockey ball is repeatedly dropped from a definite height onto the floor, it is observed that each time the ball takes the same time to come in contact with the floor, but it is also observed that the maximum height to which it rises in its first recoil differs almost every time (because the construction of a cricket or a hockey ball is nonuniform throughout, both internally and externally, and every time when the ball is dropped, different portion of its surface comes in contact with the floor during the first collision).

Now if the ball is repeatedly dropped from a definite height in such a way that each time same portion of its surface faces the floor at the instant it is dropped and it does not rotate in the air during its fall, it is observed that each time not only does it take the same time to reach the floor but it also rises to the same height in its first recoil (because now each time the same portion of its surface comes in contact with the floor during the first collision).

This example also exhibits the well-known fact that

> Relative to a reference frame, as the similarity of performances of an experiment goes on increasing, the similarity between the sets of totality of observations corresponding to the performances too goes on increasing.

It means that

> Relative to a reference frame, if an experiment be performed repeatedly in the same way (to the ultimate limit, not only in macroscopic but in microscopic terms), the sets of totality of observations corresponding to all the performances will be the same (to the ultimate limit, not only in macroscopic but in microscopic terms). ... (B.20)

The principle underlying the above statement (B.20) is what I term *principle of experiment.* Statement (B.20) can also be stated as follows:

> Relative to a reference frame, if an experiment be performed in a way that is definite to the ultimate limit (not only in macroscopic but in microscopic terms), the set of totality of observations corresponding to the performance is predestined (not only in macroscopic but in microscopic terms). ... (B.21)

This (B.21) is another expression of the principle of experiment. Let the above two statements, (B.20) and (B.21), be respectively termed *definition 1* and *definition 2 of the principle of experiment.*

B.7 APPLYING THE PRINCIPLE OF EXPERIMENT

Suppose that

1. There is an infinitely large space *S* whose total content, which at any instant can primarily be only a partino or a group of partinos, is denoted by *C*.
2. (a) Relative to a reference frame, at any instant, C can be made to have a definite identity.
   (b) Relative to a reference frame, for any timespan, C can be allowed to remain uninfluenced from everything other than itself.

... (B.22)

Since S is infinitely large or boundless (B.22-1), no partino contained by S or constituting C can ever escape from S. Thus, relative to a reference frame, throughout the time C is allowed to remain uninfluenced from everything other than itself, total energy equivalent of C or total energy content of S remains constant or partinos having a definite amount of total energy equivalent to them exist inside S. It means that throughout the time C is allowed to remain uninfluenced from everything other than itself, partinos and/or groups of partinos to which a TRF defined with respect to the partinos constituting C can be transferred according to its definition will be available.

Let

1. a PTRF defined in any particular way with respect to the partinos constituting C be denoted by R_C
2. relative to R_C
   (a) any instant be denoted by t_C
   (b) the instant that lies next to t_C be denoted by t_{Cn}

Suppose that there is an experiment *E* having the following characteristics:

1. Performing E in a definite way means relative to R_C making C to have a definite identity at any instant t_C and allowing it to remain uninfluenced from everything other than itself at the next instant t_{Cn}.
2. Relative to R_C the observation corresponding to any performance of E is the set of all the observations taken of

whatever happens inside S or of the totality of phenomena exhibited by C at t_{Cn}.

... (B.23)

Statement (B.23-1) implies that if E is performed repeatedly in a definite way, it, actually, is performed in ways that are the same (to the ultimate limit). It means that

Performing E in a definite way is same as performing it in a way that is definite to the ultimate limit. ... (B.24)

From (B.21) and (B.24), it follows that

Relative to a reference frame, if E is performed in a definite way, the set of totality of observations corresponding to the performance is predestined. ... (B.25)

Keeping in view (B.23), it follows from (B.25) that

Relative to R_C, if C is made to have a definite identity at any instant t_C and then it is allowed to remain uninfluenced from everything other than itself at the next instant t_{Cn}, the observations taken of whatever occurs inside S or of the totality of phenomena exhibited by C at t_{Cn} is predestined. ... (B.26)

The above statement (B.26) stands true, even if C acquires a definite identity at t_C, uninfluenced from everything other than itself; besides, the observations taken of whatever happens inside S or the totality of phenomena exhibited by C at any instant are representative of all the phenomena that occur inside S or that are exhibited by C at that instant. Keeping this in view, it (B.26) can be restated as

Relative to R_C, if C has a definite identity at t_C and it remains uninfluenced from everything other than itself from t_C to t_{Cn}, all the phenomena that are exhibited by C or that occur inside S at t_{Cn} are predestined. ... (B.27)

From the definition of identity (B.5) and (B.22-1), it follows that

At any instant t relative to a reference frame R, the identity of C is complete as well as exact description of C, phenomena exhibited by C, or whatever happens inside S.

Keeping this in view, (B.27) can be stated as

> Relative to R_C, if C has a definite identity at t_C and it remains uninfluenced from everything other than itself from t_C to t_{Cn}, it acquires predestined identity at t_{Cn}. ... (B.28)

Further,

Let

1. a PTRF defined in any particular way with respect to the partinos constituting G (B.11-2) or contained by V (B.11-1) be denoted by R_G
2. relative to R_G
   (a) any instant be denoted by t_G
   (b) the instant that lies next to t_G be denoted by t_{Gn}
   (c) an instant that lies in any timespan after t_G be denoted by t_{G+}
   (d) the instants that lie between t_{Gn} and t_{G+} be denoted by t_1, t_2, t_3... t_{n-2}, t_{n-1}, and t_n respectively

... (B.29)

Obviously,

> It is just (B.22-2) that makes C (B.22-1) different from G (B.11-2), or if (B.22-2) does not characterise C, C is same as G. ... (B.30)

Besides,

> Statement (B.28) stands true for C, whether (B.22-2) characterises C or not, or it is true for C, even if (B.22-2) ceases to characterise C. ... (B.31)

From (B.30) and (B.31), it follows that the basic principle stated in (B.28) for C stands true for G too:

> Relative to R_G, if G has a definite identity at t_G and it remains uninfluenced from everything other than itself from t_G to t_{Gn}, it acquires predestined identity at t_{Gn}. ... (B.32.1)

Relative to R_G, since (B.32.1) stands true for G for any two consecutive instants t_G and t_{Gn}, it stands true for the pairs of consecutive instants

t_{Gn} and t_1, t_1 and t_2, t_2 and t_3, t_{n-1} and t_n, and t_n and t_{G+}:

> Relative to R_G, if G has a definite identity at t_{Gn} and it remains uninfluenced from everything other than itself from t_{Gn} to t_1, it acquires predestined identity at t_1. ... (B.32.2)
>
> Relative to R_G, if G has a definite identity at t_1 and it remains uninfluenced from everything other than itself from t_1 to t_2, it acquires predestined identity at t_2. ... (B.32.3)
>
> Relative to R_G, if G has a definite identity at t_2 and it remains uninfluenced from everything other than itself from t_2 to t_3, it acquires predestined identity at t_3. ... (B.32.4)
>
> Relative to R_G, if G has a definite identity at t_{n-1} and it remains uninfluenced from everything other than itself from t_{n-1} to t_n, it acquires predestined identity at t_n. ... (B.32.n+1)

and

> Relative to R_G, if G has a definite identity at t_n and it remains uninfluenced from everything other than itself from t_n to t_{G+}, it acquires predestined identity at t_{G+}. ... (B.32.n+2)

From (B.32.1) and (B.32.2), it follows that

> Relative to R_G, if G has a definite identity at t_G and it remains uninfluenced from everything other than itself from t_G to t_1, it acquires predestined identities in a predestined sequence from t_{Gn} to t_1. ... (B.33)

and from (B.32.3) and (B.33), it follows that

> Relative to R_G, if G has a definite identity at t_G and it remains uninfluenced from everything other than itself from t_G to t_2, it acquires predestined identities in a predestined sequence from t_{Gn} to t_2. ... (B.34)

Statement (B.34) has been deduced from (B.32.3) and (B.33), but since (B.33) has been deduced from (B.32.1) and (B.32.2), it (B.34) has primarily come from (B.32.1), (B.32.2), and (B.32.3). In the same way as (B.33) follows from (B.32.1) and (B.32.2) and (B.34) follows from (B.32.1), (B.32.2), and (B.32.3), it follows from (B.32.1), (B.32.2), (B.32.3) ... (B.32.

n+1), and (B.32.n+2) that

> Relative to R_G, if G has a definite identity at t_G and it remains uninfluenced from everything other than itself from t_G to t_{G+}, it acquires predestined identities in a predestined sequence from t_{Gn} to t_{G+}. ... (B.35)

The above statement (B.35) can also be stated as

> Relative to R_G, if G has a definite identity at t_G and it remains uninfluenced from everything other than itself from t_G to t_{G+}, it acquires predestined identities in a predestined sequence throughout the whole of or any fraction of or predestined identity at any instant in the timespan t_{Gn} to t_{G+}. ... (B.36)

Keeping in view (B.29) and (B.12), (B.36) can also be stated as

> Relative to a PTRF R_G defined in any particular way solely with respect to the partinos constituting the content G of an infinitely large space V, if G has a definite identity at any instant t_G and it remains uninfluenced from everything other than itself from t_G to an instant that lies any timespan after t_G (t_{G+}),
>
> 1. G acquires
>   (a) predestined identities in a predestined sequence throughout the whole of or any fraction of or
>   (b) predestined identity at any instant in
>   the timespan t_{Gn} to t_{G+}.
>
> or
>
> 2. Predestined events are exhibited by G or take place inside V
>   (a) throughout the whole of or any fraction of or
>   (b) at any instant in
>   the timespan t_{Gn} to t_{G+}.
>
> ... (B.37)

If you observe the above statement (B.37) carefully, you can notice the principle of consecutive frames (5.6) underlying it.

B.8 THE PROOF

Let

1. a PTRF defined in any particular way with respect to the partinos (a series of partinos and/or groups of partinos) constituting the universe be denoted by R_u
2. relative to R_u
   (a) any instant be denoted by t_u
   (b) the instant next to t_u be denoted by t_{un}
   (c) an instant that lies any timespan after t_u be denoted by t_{u+}
   (d) any instant of the past be denoted by t_{ux}
   (e) the instant next to t_{ux} be denoted by t_{uxn}
   (f) an instant that lies any timespan after t_{ux} be denoted by t_{ux+}
   (g) the last instant of the past be denoted by t_{uxl}
   (h) the present instant be denoted by t_{up}
   (i) an instant that lies any timespan after t_{up}, that is, any instant of the future, be denoted by t_{uf}
   (j) the instant next to t_{up}, that is, the first instant of the future, be denoted by t_{ufi}
   (k) the last instant of the future if R_u is not eternal or an instant that appears infinite time after the present instant if R_u is eternal be denoted by t_{ufl}

Since the universe lies in the category of G (B.14), the principle of consecutive frames expressed in statement (B.37) for G stands true for the universe too:

> Relative to R_u, if the universe has a definite identity at t_u and it remains uninfluenced from everything other than itself from t_u to t_{u+}, it acquires predestined identities in a predestined sequence from t_{un} to t_{u+}. ... (B.38)

There exists nothing corporeal except the universe. Therefore, it can never be influenced by anything other than itself, or it always remains uninfluenced from everything other than itself. Keeping this in view, (B.38) can be stated as

> Relative to R_u, if the universe has a definite identity at t_u, it acquires predestined identities in a predestined sequence from t_{un} to t_{u+}. ... (B.39)

As a matter of fact,

> Relative to a reference frame defined in any particular way with respect to a constituent or a group of constituents of the universe, the universe had a definite identity at any instant in the past and has a definite identity at the present instant. ... (B.40)

Up to the present, R_u is formed by a definite series of such reference frames for which (B.40) stands true, so (B.40) is true for R_u too:

> Relative to R_u the universe
>
> 1. had a definite identity at any instant in the past t_{ux}
> 2. has a definite identity at the present instant t_{up}
>
> ... (B.41)

From (B.39) and (B.41-1), it follows that

> Relative to R_u the universe acquires predestined identities in a predestined sequence from t_{uxn} to t_{ux+}. ... (B.42)

Since the timespan t_{uxn} to t_{uxl} lies in the category of the timespan t_{uxn} to t_{ux+}, statement (B.42), which stands true for the latter, is true for the former too:

> Relative to R_u the universe acquires predestined identities in a predestined sequence from t_{uxn} to t_{uxl}.

or as

> Relative to a PTRF defined in any particular way with respect to the partinos constituting the universe R_u, the universe acquired predestined identities in a predestined sequence throughout the whole of or any fraction of or predestined identity at any instant in
>
> - a timespan that began just after any instant of the past t_{ux} and ended at its last instant t_{uxl} or
> - the portion of the past that appeared after, followed, or was preceded by any instant
>
> (t_{uxn} to t_{uxl}). ... (B.43)

Statement (B.42) can also be stated as

Relative to R_u the universe acquires predestined identities in a predestined sequence during a timespan preceded by any instant of the past t_{ux} (t_{uxn} to t_{ux+}). ... (B.44)

Moreover,

Relative to R_u, if past exists, the instant at present t_{up} is a timespan of unit length preceded by the last instant of the past t_{uxl}. ... (B.45)

From (B.44) and (B.45), it follows that

Relative to a PTRF defined in any particular way with respect to the partinos constituting the universe R_u, if the present instant t_{up} is preceded by any instant of the past or if past exists, the universe has acquired a predestined identity at present t_{up}. ... (B.46)

From (B.39) and (B.41-2), it follows that

Relative to R_u the universe acquires predestined identities in a predestined sequence from t_{ufi} to t_{uf}. ... (B.47)

Since the timespan t_{ufi} to t_{ufl} lies in the category of the timespan t_{ufi} to t_{uf}, statement (B.47), which stands true for the latter, is true for the former too:

Relative to R_u the universe acquires predestined identities in a predestined sequence from t_{ufi} to t_{ufl}. ... (B.48)

Relative to R_u the timespan t_{ufi} to t_{ufl} represents the whole future, whether R_u is eternal or not. Thus, (B.48) can also be stated as

Relative to a PTRF defined in any particular way with respect to the partinos constituting the universe R_u, the universe will acquire predestined identities in a predestined sequence throughout the whole of or any fraction of or predestined identity at any instant in the future (t_{ufi} to t_{ufl}). ... (B.49)

Keeping in view (B.15), the three statements (B.43), (B.46), and (B.49) can be stated respectively as

Relative to a PTRF defined in any particular way with respect to

> the partinos constituting the universe R_u, predestined phenomena, events, or happenings were exhibited by or took place in the universe throughout the whole of, throughout any fraction of, or at any instant in
>
> - a timespan that began just after any instant of the past t_{ux} and ended at its last instant t_{uxl} or
> - the portion of the past that appeared after, followed, or was preceded by any instant
>
> (t_{uxn} to t_{uxl}). ... (B.50)
>
> Relative to a PTRF defined in any particular way with respect to the partinos constituting the universe R_u, if the present instant t_{up} is preceded by any instant of the past or if past exists, predestined phenomena, events, or happenings have been exhibited by or have taken place in the universe at present t_{up}. ... (B.51)

and

> Relative to a PTRF defined in any particular way with respect to the partinos constituting the universe R_u, predestined phenomena, events, or happenings will be exhibited by or will take place in the universe throughout the whole of, throughout any fraction of, or at any instant in the future (t_{ufi} to t_{ufl}). ... (B.52)

In simple words, these three statements [(B.50), (B.51), and (B.52)] can together be stated as

> Relative to a PTRF defined in any particular way with respect to the partinos constituting the universe,
>
> 1. After any instant, the past was predestined.
> 2. If past exists, the present is predestined.
> 3. The future is predestined.
>
> ... (B.53)

A reference frame defined in any particular way with respect to only one partino or only one group of partinos is the simplest type of TRF. It is also the simplest type of PTRF, a PTRF having only one carrier, because it is defined once and for all with respect to its carrier, and therefore (B.53), which is true for a PTRF, is true for it too:

Relative to a reference frame defined in any particular way with respect to any partino or any group of partinos constituting the universe,

1. After any instant, the past was predestined.
2. If past exists, the present is predestined.
3. The future is predestined.

... (B.54)

The scientifically proven statement (B.52), which is stated in a bit simple and course form as (B.53-3) and whose deduce is (B.54-3), is the theorem of destiny (B.1) stated in a scientific form. Thus, with the proof of (B.52), the theorem of destiny is proved scientifically.

C

EXPLANATION DEMANDED ON THE BASIS OF THE PRINCIPLE OF INDETERMINACY

If you begin with probability, probability is what you end with.

MANY PHYSICISTS RAISE OBJECTIONS AGAINST THE DEFINITENESS OF THE corporeal world and therefore the predeterminedness of the future on the basis of the principle of indeterminacy. In this appendix, I have shown the invalidity of these objections by explaining the real meaning of the principle in reference to the corporeal world and, taking the traditional microscope and diffraction examples, by showing the ways in which it is being misinterpreted and misused. It requires graduate-level knowledge of physics for being understood.

C.1 PARTINO FROM BORN'S POINT OF VIEW

According to Max Born,

1. A partino (see section B.2) is physically nothing except a discrete particle.
2. At any instant relative to a reference frame, the probability that this discrete particle acquires a position is proportional to the value of $|\Psi|^2$ for that position (Ψ is the wave function

corresponding to the particle.).

... (C.1)

C.2 A CONCEPTION ABOUT DEFINITENESS

Most people think that

> It follows basically from Born's physical interpretation of Ψ and directly from the principle of indeterminacy, an offshoot of the former, that at any instant relative to a reference frame, everything from a partino to the whole universe has an uncertain or indefinite identity to at least some extent. ... (C.2)

People reach this conclusion (C.2) in numerous ways. The most common as well as seemingly convincing one is given here as an example:

Example C.1

According to the principle of indeterminacy,

> At any instant in a definite direction relative to a reference frame,
>
> - The minimum value of the product of uncertainties in the position and momentum of a particle is $h/4\pi$.
> - As the uncertainty in the position of the particle increases, the uncertainty in its momentum decreases, and vice versa.
>
> ... (C.3)

It (C.3) means that

> It is impossible for a particle to have both an absolutely definite position and an absolutely definite momentum at any instant in a definite direction relative to a reference frame. ... (C.4)

It can be said on the basis of (B.5) that

> At any instant relative to a reference frame, the identity of a particle is the set of all its properties, attributes, qualities, or characteristics, essentially including both its position and its momentum.

Keeping this in view, it follows from (C.4) that

> At any instant relative to a reference frame, it is impossible for a particle to have an absolutely definite identity. ... (C.5)

Keeping in view (B.5), it follows from (C.1-1) that

> At any instant relative to a reference frame, the identity of a partino is the identity of the associated particle.

Considering this, it follows from (C.5) that

> At any instant relative to a reference frame, it is impossible for a partino to have an absolutely definite identity. ... (C.6)

Keeping in view (B.9) and (B.10), it follows from (C.6) that

> At any instant relative to a reference frame, it is impossible for anything from a partino to the whole universe to have an absolutely definite identity.

Thus, it follows basically from the Born's physical interpretation of Ψ and directly from the principle of indeterminacy, an offshoot of the former, that

> At any instant relative to a reference frame, everything from a partino to the whole universe has an indefinite identity to at least some extent.

This is just an example of how people conclude (C.2) or conclude that indefiniteness is inherent in every corporeal thing.

C.3 THE OBJECTION

People who have this conception (C.2) naturally as well as invariably object to the proof of the theorem of destiny given in the previous appendix (Appendix B). Although they reach (C.2) through different ways, they object to the proof of the theorem of destiny in almost the same way:

From (C.2) it follows that

> At any instant relative to a reference frame, it is impossible for the universe to have an absolutely definite identity.

Therefore,

> It is impossible that the universe had an absolutely definite identity at any instant in the past or has an absolutely definite identity at present relative to a reference frame.

It means that statement (B.40) is wrong. Thus, the proof of the theorem of destiny given in the last appendix, which uses (B.40) as a reference, is invalid.

C.4 NEED OF ARRIVING AT A CONCLUSION ABOUT THE DEFINITENESS OF THE CORPOREAL WORLD

The objection against the proof of the theorem of destiny takes (C.2) as its starting reference. Thus, before any explanation can be given against the objection, it is necessary to check whether (C.2) is valid or not.

There are numerous things related to the principle of indeterminacy about which people think that they point towards the indefiniteness of the corporeal things as it is mentioned in (C.2). In the following sections, all such things related to the principle of indeterminacy will be analysed one by one to check the validity of (C.2).

C.5 DEFINITENESS AND BORN'S PHYSICAL INTERPRETATION OF Ψ

> A preliminary examination of Born's physical interpretation of Ψ (C.1) leads to the conclusion that it is in no way against the definiteness of the position and momentum of a particle at any instant relative to a reference frame. ... (C.7)

Yet a further analysis is needed to make things clearer.

It can be said about the wave function Ψ of a particle that at any instant relative to a reference frame, in any actual or nonimaginary boundary condition, $|\Psi|^2$ is a non-zero quantity for any position at finite distance from the mean position of the particle. This, keeping in view (C.1-2), means that

> At any instant relative to a reference frame, no position at finite

> distance from the mean position of a particle is impossible for it to acquire or it is possible for a particle to acquire any position at finite distance from its mean position. ... (C.8)

The same is the case with the momentum of a particle:

> At any instant relative to a reference frame, no momentum in finite range from the mean momentum of a particle is impossible for it to acquire or it is possible for a particle to acquire any momentum in finite range from its mean momentum. ... (C.9)

It is clear that

> The above two statements, (C.8) and (C.9), do not at all deny that at any instant relative to a reference frame, a particle acquires only one definite position and only one definite momentum. ... (C.10)

Besides, they, (C.8) and (C.9), do not at all mean that at any instant relative to a reference frame, a particle acquires every position at finite distance from its mean position and every finite momentum or both the position and the momentum of a particle are indefinite, as many people conclude from them. It follows from (C.7) and (C.10) that

> Neither Born's physical interpretation of ψ (C.1) itself nor (C.8) and (C.9), which follow from it, deny that at any instant relative to a reference frame, in any boundary condition, a particle acquires only one distinct, certain, or definite position and only one distinct, certain, or definite momentum. ... (C.11)

C.6 DEFINITENESS AND THE PRINCIPLE OF INDETERMINACY

The actual statement of the principle of indeterminacy is given as follows:

> At any instant in a definite direction relative to a reference frame, the standard deviations of the position and momentum of a particle, Δx and Δp, are related with each other in such a way that

$$\Delta x\ \Delta p\ h/4\pi$$

and, as Δx increases, Δp decreases and vice versa.

... (C.12)

An examination of this, (C.12), makes it clear that

> The principle of indeterminacy does not at all talk about, deal in, or even refer to anything such as uncertainty, indefiniteness, or indeterminacy in or about the position or momentum of a particle. ... (C.13)

Yet it is mainly the principle of indeterminacy on the basis of which people think of the corporeal world having indefinite characteristics, including any particle having indefinite position and momentum.

In the actual statement of the principle of indeterminacy (C.12), Δx and Δp are defined respectively as the standard deviations of the position and momentum of a particle at any instant in a definite direction relative to a reference frame. So it is clear that

> In reference to the principle of indeterminacy, Δx and Δp do not at all mean uncertainties in or about the position and momentum of a particle respectively at any instant in a definite direction relative to a reference frame, which they are generally mistaken or misinterpreted as. ... (C.14)

It follows from (C.13) or even (C.14) that the principle of indeterminacy does not at all mean that

1. At any instant in a definite direction relative to a reference frame, the minimum value of the product of uncertainties, indefiniteness, or indeterminacies in the position and momentum of a particle is $h/4\pi$.

or

2. At any instant in a definite direction relative to a reference frame, the minimum value of the product of uncertainties, indefiniteness, or indeterminacies about the position and momentum of a particle is $h/4\pi$.

... (C.15)

which it is mostly mistaken or misinterpreted as. Besides these two most popular ones, (C.15-1) and (C.15-2), there are numerous other misinterpretations of the principle of indeterminacy, which, unlike the principle of indeterminacy, talk about, deal in, or refer to things such as uncertainties, indefiniteness, and indeterminacies in or about the position and momentum of a particle.

From many misinterpretations of the principle of indeterminacy, one of which is (C.15-1), it follows that

> At any instant relative to a reference frame, a particle cannot acquire both an absolutely definite position and an absolutely definite momentum. ... (C.16)

In the same way, from many misinterpretations, one of which is (C.15-2), it follows that

> It is impossible to be absolutely certain about both the position and the momentum of a particle at any instant relative to a reference frame. ... (C.17)

People take these two statements, (C.16) and (C.17), especially (C.16), as denial of the definiteness of the position and momentum of a particle at any instant relative to a reference frame. They, (C.16) and (C.17), are outcome of the two types of misinterpretations of the principle of indeterminacy such as (C.15-1) and (C.15-2) respectively; none of them follows from or can be derived from the actual statement of the principle of indeterminacy (C.12). In short,

> Taken as denial of the definiteness of the position and momentum of a particle at any instant relative to a reference frame, statements (C.16) and (C.17) are offshoots of two types of misinterpretations of the principle of indeterminacy such as (C.15-1) and (C.15-2) respectively, not of the principle of indeterminacy (C.12). ... (C.18)

From (C.18) or even (C.13), it follows that

> The principle of indeterminacy (C.12) does not at all deny that at any instant relative to a reference frame, a particle acquires only one definite position and only one definite momentum. ... (C.19)

C.7 PHYSICAL SIGNIFICANCE OF THE PRINCIPLE OF INDETERMINACY

Largely, the principle of indeterminacy (C.12) is a statistical statement, and this is why, for people, it is so difficult to use and so easy to misinterpret. Its physical significance is worth analysing in greater detail to know what it says about the definiteness of the position and momentum of a particle at any instant relative to a reference frame.

Suppose that there is a number P that satisfies the following relation:

$$0 \leq P \leq 1$$

Now let, at any instant in a definite direction relative to a reference frame,

1. the mean position and the mean momentum of a particle be denoted by x_0 and p_0 respectively
2. the distance bisected by x_0 and the minimum distance for which the probability that the particle acquires any position in them is P [($P \times 100$) per cent] be denoted by Δx_p and Δx_m respectively
3. the range of momentum bisected by p_0 and the minimum range of momentum for which the probability that the particle acquires any momentum in them is P [($P \times 100$) per cent] be denoted by Δp_p and Δp_m respectively

To explain the significance of the principle of indeterminacy, I have introduced Δx_p, Δp_p, Δx_m, and Δp_m here because they are easier to visualise than are Δx and Δp, mentioned in statement (C.12).

Δx_p, Δp_p, Δx_m, and Δp_m are zero when P is zero; they are non-zero for all non-zero values of P; and they are almost infinite when P is equal to one. Δx_p, Δp_p, Δx_m, Δp_m, Δx, and Δp are related with each other as follows:

1. (a) Δx_p, Δx_m, and Δx increase and decrease together, and so do Δp_p, Δp_m, and Δp.
   (b) As Δx_p, Δx_m, Δx increase, Δp_p, Δp_m, and Δp decrease, and vice versa.

   The above two relations are true generally, not always—the chances of their being followed increases with the increase in the value of P or with the increase in the resemblance of the position and momentum distribution curves of the particle with the Gaussian-function curve.

2. When the position and momentum distribution curves of the particle are described exactly by the Gaussian function,

$$\Delta x_p \, \Delta p_p = \Delta x_m \, \Delta p_m = r(\Delta x \, \Delta p) = r(h/4\pi)$$

where

- $0 \leq r \leq \infty$
- For every value of P, there is a unique value of r (For example, when P is 0, 0.383, 0.683, 0.954, and 1, the values of r are 0, 1, 4, 16, and ∞ respectively.).

... (C.20)

This statement (C.20) gives a larger picture of the physical significance of the principle of indeterminacy. Obviously, like the statement of the principle of indeterminacy (C.12), it does not deny that at any instant relative to a reference frame, a particle acquires only one distinct position and only one distinct momentum. Thus,

> Whatever the principle of indeterminacy signifies for the corporeal world does not at all deny that at any instant relative to a reference frame, a particle acquires only one definite position and only one definite momentum. ... (C.21)

C.8 DEFINITENESS AND PRINCIPLE OF UNAVOIDABLE ERRORS

Let, at any instant in a definite direction relative to a reference frame,

1. the unavoidable inaccuracy or error considered in the measurement of the position and momentum of a particle be denoted by Δx_e and Δp_e respectively.
2. the unavoidable inaccuracy or error considered in the measurement of the angular position and the angular momentum of the particle be denoted by $\Delta \theta_e$ and ΔJ_e respectively.

... (C.22)

As it is obvious from their definitions, Δx_e and Δp_e are not same as Δx and Δp respectively, and therefore it is absurd to say that

$$\Delta x_e \, \Delta p_e \geq h/4\pi \qquad \text{... (C.23)}$$

which most people do on the pattern of the statement of the principle of indeterminacy, mistaking Δx_e and Δp_e as Δx and Δp respectively—most people misinterpret this erroneous statement (C.23) as the principle of indeterminacy. [In reference to the definiteness of the corporeal world, it (C.23) will be analysed in the next section.]

In the case of measurement of the position and momentum of a particle with the help of a microscope, it stands true that

$$\Delta x_e \, \Delta p_e \geq h$$

and, as Δx_e increases, Δp_e decreases and vice versa.
... (C.24)

Let the principle underlying this statement (C.24) be termed *principle of unavoidable errors*. The principle of unavoidable errors, in the same way as it governs the determination of the position and momentum of a particle, stands true for the simultaneous measurement or determination of many other pairs of properties of a particle relative to a reference frame. For example, for the determination of the angular position and the angular momentum of a particle at any instant relative to a reference frame, it is expressed as follows:

$$\Delta \theta_e \, \Delta J_e \geq h$$

and as $\Delta \theta_e$ increases, ΔJ_e decreases, and vice versa.

From the observation of (C.24), an expression of the principle of unavoidable errors, it is obvious that

> The principle of unavoidable errors does not object to the definiteness of the position and momentum of a particle at any instant relative to a reference frame. ... (C.25)

Instead, it follows from the principle of unavoidable errors (C.24) that

> At any instant relative to a reference frame, both the position

> and the momentum of a particle cannot be determined with perfect accuracy. ... (C.26)

Something cannot be determined or measured accurately does not mean that it itself has indefinite character, and this is why statement (C.26) does not mean that

> At any instant relative to a reference frame, it is impossible for a particle to acquire both a definite position and a definite momentum.

or

> Statement (C.26), which expresses a physical significance of the principle of unavoidable errors, does not deny that at any instant relative to a reference frame, a particle can have only one definite position and only one definite momentum. ... (C.27)

It follows from (C.27) or even (C.25) that

> The principle of unavoidable errors does not deny that at any instant relative to a reference frame, a particle can have only one definite position and only one definite momentum. ... (C.28)

C.9 DEFINITENESS AND MISINTERPRETATIONS OF THE PRINCIPLE OF INDETERMINACY

In the scientific world, nothing is more misinterpreted than the principle of indeterminacy. The actual statement of the principle of indeterminacy (C.12) is rarely used; mostly people use its misinterpretations that are numerous in number. Unlike the principle of indeterminacy, its almost every misinterpretation talks about, deals in, or refers to things such as uncertainties, indefiniteness, or indeterminacies in or about the position and momentum of a particle. Two most widely used misinterpretations are given here as examples:

> At any instant in a definite direction relative to a reference frame, the minimum value of the product of uncertainties or indefiniteness in the position and momentum of a particle is $h/4\pi$. ... (C.29)

and

> At any instant in a definite direction relative to a reference frame, the minimum value of the product of uncertainties, indefiniteness, or indeterminacies about the position and momentum of a particle is $h/4\pi$. ... (C.30)

The principle of indeterminacy (C.12) is theoretically proved, whereas none of its misinterpretations has any proof. They all (the misinterpretations of the principle of indeterminacy) are invalid statements. This raises an important question about them: how does anyone find or show any of the misinterpretations to be correct? Not without making a series of fallacies and mistakes. I have explained as well as exemplified this in the following subsections, taking the cases of the two aforementioned, most widely used, misinterpretations of the principle of indeterminacy, (C.29) and (C.30). But before that, to avoid wordiness, let

- a person who takes (C.29) as the principle of indeterminacy be termed α
- a person who takes (C.30) as the principle of indeterminacy be termed β

C.9.1 *How α finds his interpretation of the principle of indeterminacy to be correct?*

α makes numerous mistakes in finding and showing his interpretation of the principle of indeterminacy (C.29) to be correct.

He starts with erroneously defining 'standard deviation' as 'uncertainty'. Then, in any example that he gives to show the validity of (C.29), what he selects as uncertainties in the position and momentum of a particle at any instant in any particular direction relative to a reference frame, say Δx_u and Δp_u, are different from its standard deviations Δx and Δp respectively—he selects minimum ranges of position and momentum in which there is respectively about ninety-five and eighty per cent probability of finding the particle. Thus, as the value of the product of Δx_u and Δp_u, he gets h, which is approximately thirteen times the minimum possible value of Δx and Δp, $h/4\pi$.

Getting the value of h for $\Delta x_u\, \Delta p_u$, that is, getting the value of h for the product of what he interprets as Δx and Δp basically, α compares it with $h/4\pi$ and, finding it larger than the latter, thinks that the validity of the statement (C.29) is proved or the principle of indeterminacy is being followed. This comparison is absurd because, in the principle of indeterminacy, $h/4\pi$ is given as the minimum possible value of the product of Δx and Δp and what α takes as Δx and Δp, Δx_u and Δp_u, are different from Δx and Δp respectively.

In this sequence he makes another basic mistake of interpretation. He ignores that to show the validity of (C.29), it is not enough to show that $\Delta x_u \, \Delta p_u > h/4\pi$ but it is necessary to show that $(\Delta x_u \, \Delta p_u)_{min} = h/4\pi$.

α mostly uses the case of single slit diffraction of electrons to show the validity of his interpretation of the principle of indeterminacy (C.29). Now, with the analysis of the same experiment, I shall show you how α uses this erroneous method to find (C.29) to be correct, how wrong his interpretation of the principle of indeterminacy is, and how closely the actual statement of the principle of indeterminacy is being followed.

Example C.2

In the case of Fraunhofer diffraction of electrons through a narrow slit, let

1. a reference frame fixed with respect to the slit be denoted by R_s
2. relative to R_s, the slit width be denoted by s
3. a line that lies in the plane of, passes through the centre of, and is perpendicular to the length of the slit be denoted by L
4. a point that lies on L on or between the edges of the slit be denoted by W and its distance from one edge of the slit in the positive direction be denoted by y
5. a typical electron that is made to take part in the experiment be denoted by e
6. the wavelength of e be denoted by λ
7. the ratio of s to λ be denoted by n
8. relative to R_s, along L,
   (a) the wave function of e be denoted by ψ_e
   (b) the standard deviations of the position and momentum of e be denoted by Δx_{el} and Δp_{el} respectively
9. a screen parallel to the plane of the slit and kept in front of it at a very large distance from it be denoted by N
10. a line on N that is parallel to and lies closest to L be denoted by L_2
11. a line that passes through the centre of the slit and perpendicularly intersects both L and L_2 be denoted by L_0

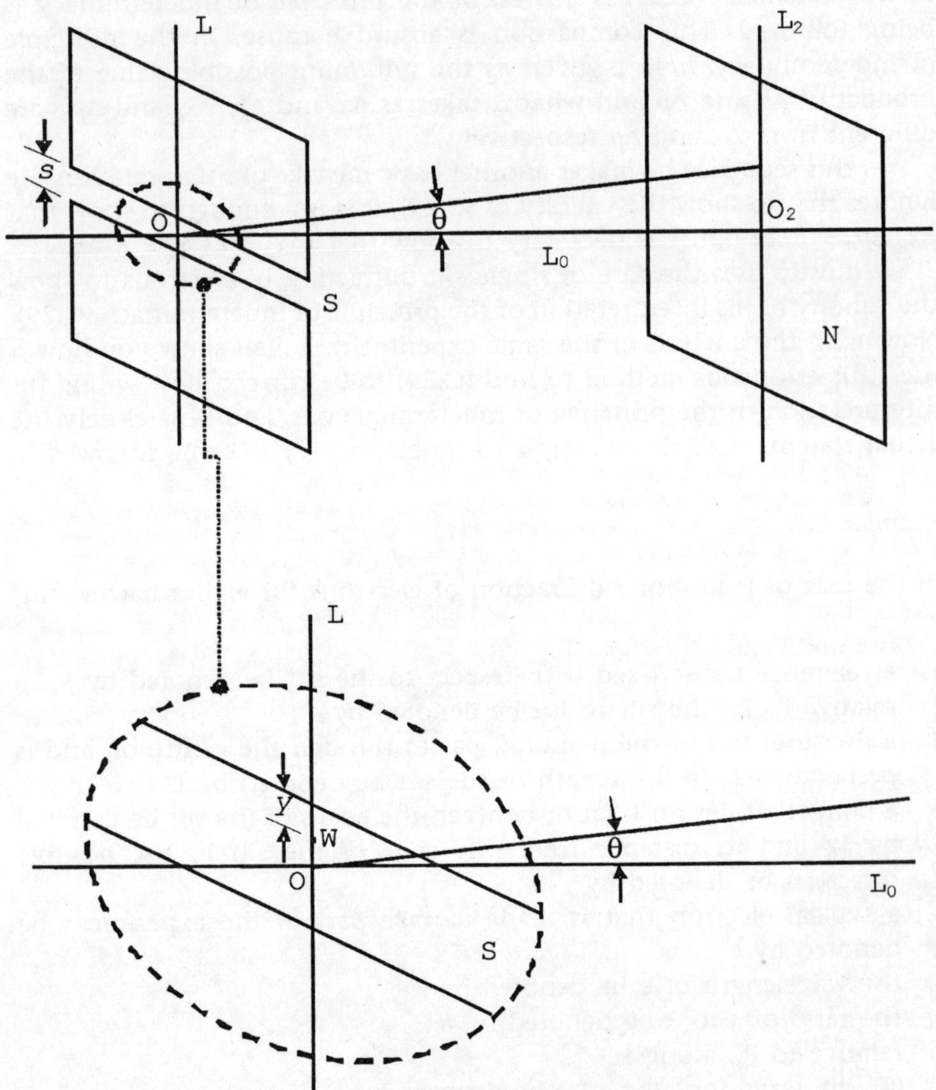

Figure C.1

12. the points where L_0 intersects L and L_2 be denoted by O and O_2 respectively
13. relative to R_s, along L_0, the momentum of e be denoted by p_{el0}
14. the intensity of electron beam on the screen at any point on L_2 and at O_2 be denoted by I and I_0 respectively

15. the angle that a line passing through O and through any point on L_2 makes with L_0 be denoted by θ
16. relative to R_s, along L_2,
    (a) the range of momentum of diffracted electrons that is half of the range of momentum of electrons forming the central maxima on the screen and that has the momentum at O_2, zero momentum, at its centre be denoted by Δp_{elm}
    (b) the momentum wave function and standard deviation of momentum of e be denoted by ψ_{ep2} and Δp_{el2} respectively

Applying the principle of indeterminacy (C.12), relative to R_s, the minimum possible value of the product of standard deviations of position and momentum of e along L at the instant it passes through the plane of the slit, $(\Delta x_{el}\ \Delta p_{el})_{\min}$, is $h/4\pi$:

$$\Delta x_{el}\ \Delta p_{el} \geq h/4\pi \qquad \text{... (C.31)}$$

The very first mistake that α makes is that, instead of using the definite terms 'standard deviation of position' and 'standard deviation of momentum' of the actual statement of the principle of indeterminacy, he uses absurd terms 'uncertainty in position' and 'uncertainty in momentum' respectively.

As uncertainties in the position and momentum of e in the direction of L when it passes through the plane of the slit relative to R_s, basically as Δx_{el} and Δp_{el}, α takes s and Δp_{elm} respectively. Using the wave theory of diffraction and De Broglie's expression for particle wavelength, he rightly shows that

$$s\ \Delta p_{elm} = h \qquad \text{... (C.32)}$$

A deeper analysis is needed to see whether s and Δp_{elm} are related in any way to Δx_{el} and Δp_{el}.

While e passes through the plane of the slit, its wave function at any point along L on or between the edges of the slit can be described closely by considering it passing between infinitely hard walls separated by a distance s:

$$\psi_e \approx (2/s)^{1/2} \sin 2n\pi y/s$$

Thus, its standard deviation along L is given as

$$\Delta x_{el} \approx s\{1/12 + [(\sin 4n\pi)(1 - 2n^2\pi^2) - 2n\pi\ (1 + \cos 4n\pi)]/32n^3\pi^3\}^{1/2} \qquad \text{... (C.33)}$$

In reality, no wall is infinitely hard. So, along L, there is always some possibility, five per cent roughly, of finding e outside the walls of the slit. Therefore, ψ_e has some, very small, magnitude beyond the walls, and the actual value of the standard deviation of e is slightly higher than the approximate value given by (C.33), which is exact enough for the current analysis. Also, that e cannot be confined hundred per cent within the walls of the slit along L shows again that α is incorrect in using 'uncertainty in position' for the slit width.

According to De Broglie, the momentum of e along L_0 is related to its wavelength as follows:

$$p_{el0} = h/\lambda \qquad \text{... (C.34)}$$

Besides, through optics, it can be shown that

$$p_{el0} = n \, \Delta p_{elm} \qquad \text{... (C.35)}$$

and

$$I = I_0[(sin \; \gamma)/\gamma]^2 \qquad \text{... (C.36)}$$

where $\gamma = n\pi \sin \theta$. The momentum wave function of e on the screen in the direction of L_2 can be derived from the above intensity-distribution expression (C.36):

$$\psi_{ep2} = (\text{Sin } \gamma)/\{4\gamma^2 n \, \Delta p_{elm} \, [1/2! - (2n\pi)^2/(3 \times 4!) + (2n\pi)^4/(5 \times 6!) - (2n\pi)^6/(7 \times 8!) ...]\}^{1/2} \qquad \text{... (C.37)}$$

From (C.37) it can be shown that Δp_{elm} is the minimum range of momentum in the direction of L relative to R_s for which the probability that e acquires any momentum in it when it is incident on the screen or when it passes through the plane of the slit ranges from about eighty-six per cent, for $n = 1$, to seventy-seven per cent, for $n >> 1$. This gives an alternate meaning to what α has chosen as uncertainty in the momentum of e in the direction of L and shows again how wrong he is in using 'uncertainty' here.

With the help of the same statement (C.37), we can also determine the standard deviation of the momentum of e on the screen in the direction of L_2:

$$\Delta p_{el2} = (\Delta p_{elm}/2\pi)/\{[1 - (\text{Sin } 2n\pi)/2n\pi]/[1/2! - (2n\pi)^2/(3 \times 4!) + (2n\pi)^4/(5 \times 6!) - (2n\pi)^6/(7 \times 8!) ...]\}^{1/2} \qquad \text{... (C.38)}$$

Since the momentum of any electron during its journey from the slit to the screen remains almost unchanged, the standard deviation of the momentum of e at the slit along L is same as it is on the screen along L_2, that is,

$$\Delta p_{el} = \Delta p_{el2} \quad \text{... (C.39)}$$

From (C.38) and (C.39), it follows that

$$\Delta p_{el} = (\Delta p_{elm}/2\pi)/\{[1 - (\text{Sin } 2n\pi)/2n\pi]/[1/2! - (2n\pi)^2/(3 \times 4!) + (2n\pi)^4/(5 \times 6!) - (2n\pi)^6/(7 \times 8!)...]\}^{1/2} \quad \text{... (C.40)}$$

Statements (C.33) and (C.40) express how Δx_{el} and Δp_{el} depend on s and Δp_{elm} respectively. During this experiment s, and therefore Δp_{elm} (C.32), is varied, whereas λ, and therefore p_{el0} (C.34), is kept constant. So it is also important to see how Δx_{el} and Δp_{el} are related to λ and p_{el0} respectively. Keeping in view that $s = n\lambda$, we can restate (C.33) as

$$\Delta x_{el} \approx n\lambda\{1/12 + [(\sin 4n\pi)(1 - 2n^2\pi^2) - 2n\pi\ (1+ \cos 4n\pi)]/32n^3\pi^3\}^{1/2} \quad \text{... (C.41)}$$

and from (C.35) and (C.40), it follows that

$$\Delta p_{el} = (p_{el0}/2n\pi)/\{[1 - (\text{Sin } 2n\pi)/2n\pi]/[1/2! - (2n\pi)^2/(3 \times 4!) + (2n\pi)^4/(5 \times 6!) - (2n\pi)^6/(7 \times 8!)...]\}^{1/2} \quad \text{... (C.42)}$$

From (C.33) and (C.40), we can calculate the values of Δx_{el} and Δp_{el} in terms of s and Δp_{elm} respectively for different values of n; the values of Δx_{el} and Δp_{el} in terms λ and p_{el0} respectively as a function of n can be calculated using (C.41) and (C.42); and for all these pairs of values of Δx_{el} and Δp_{el}, the values of $\Delta x_{el}\ \Delta p_{el}$ can be calculated with the aid of (C.32) or (C.34). (See table C.1 on the next page)

Keeping in view (C.33) and (C.40), it is obvious that what α selects as uncertainties in the position and momentum, s and Δp_{elm}, are different from what he should have selected according to the principle of indeterminacy (C.12), that is, standard deviations of position and momentum of e along L relative to R_s, Δx_{el} and Δp_{el}. This is the second mistake that α makes in his interpretation of the principle of indeterminacy. Besides, the values of s and Δp_{elm} relative to Δx_{el} and Δp_{el} respectively for different values of n given in table C.1 also make it clear why the value of $s\ \Delta p_{elm}$, h (C.32), is about thirteen times the minimum possible value of $\Delta x_{el}\ \Delta p_{el}$, $h/4\pi$ (C.31).

TABLE C.1 APPROXIMATE VALUES OF Δx_{el}, Δp_{el}, AND $\Delta x_{el}\ \Delta p_{el}$

n	Δx_{el}		Δp_{el}		$\Delta x_{el}\ \Delta p_{el}$
1	$s/3.76$	$\lambda/3.76$	$\Delta p_{elm}/2.99$	$p_{elO}/2.99$	$1.12h/4\pi$
2	$s/3.53$	$\lambda/1.77$	$\Delta p_{elm}/2.17$	$p_{elO}/4.34$	$1.64h/4\pi$
3	$s/3.49$	$\lambda/1.16$	$\Delta p_{elm}/1.81$	$p_{elO}/5.43$	$1.99h/4\pi$
> 3	$s/3.47$	$n\lambda/3.47$	$n^{1/2}\ \Delta p_{elm}\ /\pi$	$p_{elO}/\pi n^{1/2}$	$1.15n^{1/2}h/4\pi$

According to the principle of indeterminacy, the value of the product of Δx_{el} and Δp_{el} should be either equal to or greater than $h/4\pi$, that is, $\Delta x_{el}\ \Delta p_{el} \geq h/4\pi$. Misinterpreting s and Δp_{elm} basically as Δx_{el} and Δp_{el} respectively, α compares the value of their product, h, with the minimum possible value of the product of Δx_{el} and Δp_{el}, $h/4\pi$, and, finding it larger than the latter, says, 'See, the product of s and Δp_{elm} is greater than $h/4\pi$, so the principle of indeterminacy is being followed in this case or the validity of (C.29) is proved.' In this way he makes third and fourth mistakes simultaneously.

Since s and Δp_{elm} are different from Δx_{el} and Δp_{el} respectively [(C.33) and (C.40)], it is absurd to compare the value of their product with the minimum possible value of the product of the latter, $h/4\pi$, to show the validity of either the principle of indeterminacy or his interpretation of the principle of indeterminacy (C.29)—this is the third mistake made by α.

His fourth or final mistake is that he misinterprets the meaning of '≥' inherent in (C.29) as well as in the statement of the principle of indeterminacy. That the product of s and Δp_{elm}, h, is higher than $h/4\pi$ is not enough to show that his interpretation of indeterminacy (C.29) is valid or is being followed in this case; to show the validity of (C.29) here, it is necessary to show that the minimum possible value of the product of what he takes as uncertainties in the position and momentum of e along L relative to R_s, $(s\ \Delta p_{elm})_{min}$, is equal to $h/4\pi$. Analysis shows that for the whole valid range of n not only the value but also the minimum possible value of the product of s and Δp_{elm} is h, which is not only unequal to but 12.57 times $h/4\pi$. This result shows not that α's interpretation of the principle of indeterminacy (C.29) is valid but that it is totally invalid.

On the other hand, from the results expressed in the table C.1, it is obvious that (a) when the slit width is varied for a definite value of λ, as Δx_{el} increases, Δp_{el} decreases and vice-versa and (b) the approximate minimum value of $\Delta x_{el}\ \Delta p_{el}$, calculated for $n = 1$, is 1.12 $h/4\pi$, which is just 1.12 times its minimum possible value $h/4\pi$. This result strongly suggests that the actual statement of the principle of indeterminacy is being followed in this case; yet it is not a proof, because to prove that the actual statement of the principle of indeterminacy is being followed here, it is necessary to show that $(\Delta x_{el}\ \Delta p_{el})_{\min} = h/4\pi$.

The mistakes, misinterpretations, and fallacies that α makes in his effort of proving the validity of his interpretation of the principle of indeterminacy [the absurd statement (C.29)], which I have already pointed as well as exemplified above, are listed in brief as follows:

- use of incongruous terms 'uncertainty in position' and 'uncertainty in momentum' for 'standard deviation of position' Δx and 'standard deviation of momentum' Δp (C.12) respectively
- as Δx and Δp, selecting ranges of position and momentum (Δx_u and Δp_u) respectively that are different from Δx and Δp and that do not have any definite definition
- comparing the product of Δx_u and Δp_u, which are different from Δx and Δp respectively, with $h/4\pi$, which is the minimum possible value for the product of Δx and Δp, not the minimum possible value for the product of two any other at-random or undefined quantities
- interpreting '≥' just as 'greater than' instead of its complete meaning 'greater than or equal to'

C.9.2 *Analysing β's interpretation of the principle of indeterminacy*

For her interpretation of the principle of indeterminacy (C.30), β takes Δx_e and Δp_e (C.22-1) as uncertainties about the position and momentum of a particle respectively, or

> By her interpretation of the principle of indeterminacy (C.30), β means
>
> $$\Delta x_e\ \Delta p_e \geq h/4\pi$$
>
> which is the same as (C.23). ... (C.43)

Thus, the mistakes β does in finding (C.30) to be correct are actually those she does in finding (C.23) to be correct. Analysis shows that these mistakes are basically similar to those done by α in finding his interpretation of the principle of indeterminacy (C.29) to be correct; it would be an unnecessary repetition to point towards them here.

But it is important to analyse the validity of her interpretation of the principle of indeterminacy (C.30). I shall do this analysis with the help of an example, taking the case of the measurement of the position and momentum of a particle with the help of a. microscope, which β mostly presents to show the validity of (C.30).

Example C.3

Let

1. a reference frame fixed to the microscope be denoted by R_m
2. the aperture situated just before the objective of the microscope, from where the light reflected by the particle enters the microscope, be denoted by *A*
3. during the measurement the photon that is reflected by the particle and that enters the microscope through the aperture A be denoted by *ph*
4. the diameter of A that makes the least angle with the initial velocity of the particle be denoted by *D*
5. relative to R_m, in the direction of D,
   (a) the unavoidable inaccuracy, error, or indeterminacy in the measurement of the position and momentum of the particle be denoted by Δx_{ep} and Δp_{ep} respectively
   (b) before the particle reflects ph, the standard deviations of the position and momentum of the particle be denoted by Δx_{pa} and Δp_{pa} respectively

In this case β takes Δx_{ep} and Δp_{ep} respectively as uncertainties about the position and momentum of the particle in the direction of D relative to R_m. With the help of the laws of optics and quantum mechanics, she rightly shows that

$$\Delta x_{ep}\ \Delta p_{ep} \geq h \qquad \text{... (C.44)}$$

This result endorses the principle of unavoidable errors because it is in perfect accordance with (C.24), an expression of the principle. But what does it say about β's interpretation of the principle of indeterminacy?

β compares the minimum possible value of the product of Δx_{ep} and Δp_{ep}, h, with $h/4\pi$ and, finding it greater than the latter, gets convinced that (C.23) is being followed in this case. She is wrong because

> To show the validity of (C.23) in this example, it is essential to show that
>
> $$\Delta x_{ep}\ \Delta p_{ep} = \Delta x_{pa}\ \Delta p_{pa}$$
>
> or
>
> $$(\Delta x_{ep}\ \Delta p_{ep})_{\min} = h/4\pi \qquad \text{... (C.45)}$$

whereas, if you look into the matter, you will find that neither Δx_{ep} and Δp_{ep} have any definite relation with Δx_{pa} and Δp_{pa} respectively nor $\Delta x_{ep}\ \Delta p_{ep}$ has any definite relation with $\Delta x_{pa}\ \Delta p_{pa}$. On the contrary, Δx_{ep} and Δp_{ep} depend on the wavelength of ph and on the location of the particle with respect to the aperture of the microscope in such a way as stated already in (C.44):

$$(\Delta x_{ep}\ \Delta p_{ep})_{\min} = h$$

It means that the minimum possible value of the product of Δx_{ep} and Δp_{ep}, h, is more than twelve times $h/4\pi$, which should have been its minimum possible value if (C.23) were correct [see (C.45)]. This shows that (C.23) is invalid; and since (C.23) is what β means by (C.30) [according to (C.43)], her interpretation of the principle of indeterminacy (C.30) is also invalid.

Thus, the main mistake that β does in the process of finding her interpretation of the principle of indeterminacy (C.30), by which she means (C.23), to be correct is comparing the product of the unavoidable errors in the measurement of the position and momentum of a particle, which has no relation with the product of the standard deviations of the position and momentum of the particle, with the minimum possible value of the product of the latter ($h/4\pi$) at any instant in a definite direction relative to a reference frame.

C.9.3 *Inference*

The mistakes and fallacies done by people in proving other misinterpretations of the principle of indeterminacy to be correct are more or less the same as those done by α and β in proving their misinterpretations to be correct. From many misinterpretations, one of which is (C.29), it follows that

> At any instant relative to a reference frame, a particle cannot acquire both an absolutely definite position and an absolutely definite momentum. ... (C.46)

This statement (C.46) denies the definiteness of the position and momentum of a particle at any instant relative to a reference frame. But since all the interpretations of the principle of indeterminacy from which it follows are invalid statements, its denial on their basis is meaningless. To summarise,

> Since the misinterpretations of the principle of indeterminacy are invalid statements, none of them can be a basis for objection to the definiteness of the position and momentum of a particle at any instant relative to a reference frame. ... (C.47)

C.10 DEFINITENESS AND THE CORPOREAL WORLD

It is time now to sum up the conclusions of the last five sections and find out what the principle of indeterminacy and other things related to it say about the definiteness of the corporeal world.

Restating (C.47),

> Being invalid, the misinterpretations of the principle of indeterminacy, such as (C.29) and (C.30), cannot object to the definiteness of the position and momentum of a particle at any instant relative to a reference frame. ... (C.48)

From (C.11), (C.19), (C.21), and (C.28), it follows that

> None of the factors below deny that at any instant relative to a reference frame, a particle can have only one definite position and only one definite momentum:

- Born's physical interpretation of Ψ
- the principle of indeterminacy
- whatever the principle of indeterminacy means or signifies for the corporeal world
- the principle of unavoidable errors

... (C.49)

It follows from (C.48) and (C.49) that the conclusions reached in the last five sections [(C.11), (C.19), (C.21), (C.28), and (C.47)] can be summed up to say that

> Neither the principle of indeterminacy itself nor any physical law related to it denies that at any instant relative to a reference frame, a particle acquires only one definite position and only one definite momentum. ... (C.50)

That which has been proved from section C.5 to section C.9 and summed up in (C.50) for the position and momentum of a particle can, somewhat in the same way, also be proved and concluded for any other pair of physical quantities whose definiteness is questioned on the basis of the principle of indeterminacy, such as for energy and time or for angular position and angular momentum. It means that

> Neither the principle of indeterminacy nor any of the laws related to it can be a basis for objection to the definiteness of any of the physical quantities describing a particle or any of the properties of a particle at any instant relative to a reference frame.
> ... (C.51)

Keeping in view (B.5), it follows from (C.51) that

> Neither the principle of indeterminacy nor any of the laws related to it denies that at any instant relative to a reference frame, a particle has a definite identity. ... (C.52)

Keeping in view (B.5), it follows from (C.1-1) that

> At any instant relative to a reference frame, the identity of a partino is the identity of the associated particle. ... (C.53)

Keeping in view (C.53), it follows from (C.52) that

Neither the principle of indeterminacy nor any of the laws related to it denies that at any instant relative to a reference frame, a partino has a definite identity. ... (C.54)

Keeping in view (B.9) and (B.10), it follows from (C.54) that

Neither the principle of indeterminacy nor any of the laws related to it denies that at any instant relative to a reference frame, the universe or anything that it contains has a definite identity. ... (C.55)

The conclusion reached above (C.55) implies that

Statement (C.2) is wrong. ... (C.56)

And therefore all the ways in which (C.2) is reached as a conclusion are invalid in some way or the other. For example, the way given in example C.1 is wrong because the statement used as its starting reference (C.3) is an invalid interpretation of the principle of indeterminacy [α's misinterpretation (C.29)].

C.11 THE EXPLANATION

The observation of the objection against the proof of the theorem of destiny presented in the previous appendix (see section C.3) makes it clear that it can be valid if and only if (C.2) is correct. Now since (C.2) has been proved invalid (C.56), the objection that takes it as its starting reference too has been proved invalid.

To be more specific, it follows from (C.55) that (C.2) is incorrect or that neither the principle of indeterminacy nor any of the laws related to it can be a basis for objection to the statement (B.40), which has been used as a reference in the proof of the theorem of destiny and which is the basic target of the objection on the basis of the principle of indeterminacy. Thus, neither the principle of indeterminacy nor any of the laws related to it can be a basis for objection to the proof of the theorem of destiny and therefore to the predestinedness of the future.

D

PREDICTION OF THE FUTURE AND THE PRINCIPLE OF UNAVOIDABLE ERRORS

How far can I see through this translucent glass!

TO DETERMINE THE IDENTITY THAT THE UNIVERSE WILL HAVE AT ANY instant in the future, we need to know the identity that it has at present or had at any instant in the past relative to a reference frame. One of the reasons of this not being possible is that we are not yet sure about the structure of mave (B.2-1)—it is still a mysterious blend of particle and wave for us. Born's model of mave, a foundation stone of quantum mechanics and the root of the principle of indeterminacy, represents this ignorance of ours.

Even if we come to accurately know the construction of mave, we cannot determine the identity of the universe at any instant relative to a reference frame with perfect accuracy. One reason of this is that when the properties of any object are measured, an unpredictable change is introduced in its state unavoidably. The principle of unavoidable errors (see section C.8) represents this limitation:

In accordance with the principle of unavoidable errors,

> There are numerous pairs of properties, such as position and momentum, and angular position and angular momentum, for each of which (pairs) it stands true that relative to a reference frame, simultaneous perfectly accurate determination of both the

> member properties of a parton (B.2-2) is not possible.
> ... (D.1)

For example, from (C.24), one of the expressions of the principle of unavoidable errors in Born's language, it follows that

> At any instant relative to a reference frame, it is not possible to determine both the position and the momentum of a particle with perfect accuracy.

From (D.1) and (B.5), it follows that

> At any instant relative to a reference frame, it is not possible to determine the identity of a parton with complete accuracy.
> ... (D.2)

From (B.2) it follows that

> At any instant relative to a reference frame, at an elementary level, the universe is a group of partons and anything that it contains is either a parton or a group of partons. ... (D.3)

Keeping this (D.3) in view, it follows from (D.2) that

> At any instant relative to a reference frame, it is not possible to determine the identity of the universe or anything that it contains with perfect accuracy. ... (D.4)

As you know,

> Relative to a reference frame, of the things that are essential for complete as well as accurate prediction of the future, one is the determination of the identity of the universe at present or at any instant of the past. ... (D.5)

From (D.4) and (D.5), it follows that

> Relative to a reference frame, it is impossible to predict the future with perfect accuracy. ... (D.6)

Since (D.6) is an outcome of the principle of unavoidable errors, it can be concluded that

- That the future cannot be predicted with absolute accuracy (D.6) owes its existence to the principle of unavoidable errors.

or

- The principle of unavoidable errors poses an ultimate limit to the accuracy with which the future can be predicted.

Part B
The Author

E

HOW DID I FIND GOD?

After the midnight I woke up in a dream:
The universe was woven in a web of strings.
They pulled the planets as if they were feathers
and spun the stars as if they were tops.
Danced around smoothly in a musical flow
small to big, light to massive—one to all;
they all were slaves to the mighty strings.
With thoughts in my mind and feelings in my heart,
I was amazed and proud of my obvious freedom.
Embracing my worries, I slipped back in the slumber.

Before the dawn when I was half asleep,
I felt my body writhe in deep agony.
Now I was not different from the lifeless.
My whole being was captive to the same strings.
In the mighty grip, I also was like a toy.
My heart fluttered at their direction;
my thoughts danced at their discretion.
Shattered ego left a painful void.
Just a straw in the giant, roaring flow,
I found my freedom in absolute slavery.

I was quite awake when it was dawn.
World had changed since the last night.
It was cool—the sun had only light.
Every tree was giving the same music;
every bird was chirping the same song:

the music of flow, the song of freedom.
Every flower waved the same message;
every little dewdrop showed the same image:
the message of beautiful order, the image of almighty
God.
How effortlessly and adeptly it played with the strings!

WHEN I SAY THAT I FOUND GOD, I MEAN THAT I DID NOT READ OR HEAR anywhere but concluded myself what God is. Finding God was not my primary goal though. It is while I was trying to achieve the highest spiritual state that I realised the predestinedness of the future and came across God, as a result of a series of thoughts, experiments, and experiences, which I have described briefly in this appendix. But before that I shall answer how old or new this idea of God is, who could be termed the first to know God, and how original my work is.

E.1 AM I THE FIRST TO KNOW GOD?

I had read numerous books on religion and theology before I realised God, but I do not remember reading anywhere what I had found, that it is the set of all the laws of nature. So when I found God, I thought that I am the first to know God, but as time passed by, I discovered that other people have also been thinking about God in terms of the laws of nature.

After completing the first draft of the book, I got an Internet connection mainly to contact relevant persons while trying to get it published; though, indeed, I found the Internet much more useful. I searched the Web to see whether anyone else had recognised the set of all the laws of nature as God and found that Adib Ben Jebara has mentioned not the same but a similar thing. In a paper named 'All things are numbers', he has mentioned the possibility of God being the set of the laws of nature and the laws of ethics. In Chapter 13, I have shown why God cannot be as it is mentioned by Jebara.

I continued the search with various combinations of 'set', 'group', 'laws', 'nature', and 'God' and found a few Web pages related to philosophy and physics where it was written that for scientists God means laws of nature. Then I searched for the scientists' opinions and conclusions about God but could not find any particular scientist mentioning laws of nature as God.

Meanwhile, I read a book *God, Creation, and Contemporary Physics* by Mark William Worthing to see whether any scientist has recognised the set of all the laws of nature as God. Though the book does not mention any person or any school of thought stating the same thing, on page 66 it quotes famous scientist Steven Weinberg expressing a distant and bleak possibility of something similar:

> We would agree here with the physicist Steven Weinberg, who contends that if the word God has to retain any meaning at all—even for those who reject the idea of God's existence—"it should be taken to mean an interested God...who has established not only the laws of nature but also the standards of good and evil, some personality that is concerned with our actions [and]...is appropriate for us to worship." Any other God becomes so "abstract and unengaged that He is hardly to be distinguished from the laws of nature."[1]

Obviously, Weinberg does not recognise the laws of nature as God. He accepts them as a second possibility—first being God who is interested in human beings, who has established the laws of nature... and who is worth being worshipped. Well, there is no evidence at all of such a God as is believed by Weinberg. But surely, what he expresses as the second possibility makes some sense: 'Any other God becomes so abstract and unengaged that He is hardly to be distinguished from the laws of nature.'

Anyway, whoever expressed the possibility of the laws of nature being God has made a blunder, as she did not give it enough thought due to lack of confidence in the idea: the laws of nature cannot be God, because they are plural whereas God is singular. As the members of parliament cannot be the parliament, the laws of nature cannot be God. As I have shown, God can only be the set of all the laws of nature, which is also equivalent to the law that properly and completely represents all the laws of nature if such a law exists.

Later, I read the transcript of the interview that Stephen Hawking had given in 1999 in which he had said that he believes in God if it means the embodiment of the laws of the universe.[2] Hawking was just a step away from knowing God; God in which he believes is nothing other than what I had found, the set of all the laws of nature.

In short, I had read many books before writing mine and searched a lot while working on it but could not find anyone claiming or even expressing the possibility that God is the set of all the laws of nature, which I realised as well as proved independently and expressed in this book. This tempts me to say that I am the first to know God. But, obviously, I have not read all that has ever been written in the world about God. So whoever is the first to mention that God is, and is only, the set of all the laws of nature can be termed as the first person to know God.

This can make you ask, 'Well, may be, as you claim, you concluded yourself that God is the set of all the laws of nature, but whose idea or ideas did you take as the starting point?' Let me answer this question by putting some light on the originality of my work.

E.2 THE ORIGINALITY OF MY WORK

I read thousands of pages of religious texts to extract the summaries of what eight major theistic religions of the world say about God, which I have presented in Chapter 9. Though I did not copy them from anywhere, they cannot be said to be originally mine, because I have summarised them from the details of different religions that I had collected for the purpose. Except that and some conclusions that I have named as others', whatever proofs, analyses, and conclusions I have given in this book have resulted from my years of experimentation, observation, and thought on general religious and spiritual beliefs and scientific facts—they have not been taken, copied, or summarised from anybody else's thoughts or conclusions. Even the scientific proofs, analyses, and conclusions that I have presented in the appendices are purely original in this sense. This is true also for the finding that God is the set of all the laws of nature. I did not use any other person's thought or conclusion as starting point to recognise God.

As I said in the last section, after writing the first draft of the book, I searched the Web and read a few relevant books to see whether someone else had recognised the set of all the laws of nature as God before me. Though I could not find anyone saying the same thing, I found a number of other conclusions about God, such as those of Jebara, Weinberg, and Tipler[3]. After reading them I finally decided to write and add Chapter 13 (Why Can Any Other Being Not Be God?) to remove every trace of doubt from your mind about it and added this appendix to show you how correct I am with my claim of finding God and how I found it.

You can further ask, 'If your book is as original as you claim, how did you reach the conclusions you have presented in it?' To answer this question and to let you have a better insight into and understanding of my work, I am presenting here in brief the account of how I realised that whatever happens is predestined and that God is the set of all the laws of nature.

E.3 HOW DID I FIND GOD?

Since childhood I have taken a keen interest in religious, spiritual, mythological, and philosophical topics. Steadily developed in me an intense desire to achieve the highest spiritual state. This desire started to translate into efforts when I was about fourteen years old. Although, with the passage of time and increase in my knowledge, the definition of highest spiritual state changed for me from achievement of supernatural or paranormal powers, realisation of deity, and getting *moksh*[4] (salvation) to attaining the state of *sumadhi*[5], my efforts for it went on becoming more and more sincere.

To find out the way to achieve my goal, I continued to read books on spirituality, religion, philosophy, mysticism, occultism, and so on, including biographies of yogis, sages, ascetics, mystics, and devotees. I followed any path or method that seemed to me as leading to my goal with great passion and vigour till I continued to find it promising. What I found to be most recommended was meditation, which I had started trying to do soon after the beginning of my efforts. Among various other things with which I experimented while trying to achieve my goal, some were truth, desires, selfless work, ego, and feelings.

I tried hard for about eleven years but could not realise my aim, whether it was due to lack of proper direction or lack of effort on my part. Though I could not achieve what I had aimed at, my efforts for it were not completely futile. After a long period of struggle, it was during these efforts and experiments that I realised God and the absolute predestinedness of the future.

E.3.1 *Becoming free from the illusion of freedom of choice*

My experiment with doubt or state of indecision came as a turning point in my life. As I grew up, I noticed that I used to take great care and spend more than the normal time in taking decisions. Though it was because I wanted to get the best out of my every decision, I was not satisfied with this habit of mine, because every bit of time that I was left with after my studies I wanted to spend in meditation instead of decision making or planning for what I had to do. Besides, I had read a number of times at a number of places that doubt is a great enemy of a person who wishes to attain spiritual heights. Finally, in 1990, when I was eighteen years old, I decided to try to become completely free from the state of indecision.

Meanwhile, my experiments with truth were going on and they had already been putting me in various types of novel, difficult, weird situations demanding a lot of thought and time for making decisions. I knew that it is not possible to do anything without making a proper decision, but since I had decided to follow the path of becoming free from the state of indecision, I started trying to minimise the decision-making time so as to achieve my aim gradually. This inevitably led to the analysis of the decision-making process.

Some decisions were so important that it was not possible to finalise them in haste—I had to spend time thinking about them. But I found that not all the decisions that I made with perfect care and full thought could prove themselves worthy—some of them boomeranged or were failures on the touchstone of time. On the failure of any important decision, the question used to arise in my mind that why I had not selected any other option that was before me. In all these cases, putting myself back in the past, I found that the decision that I had made in any particular situation and time was unchangeable or inevitable, or if time is turned back and once again I encounter the same situation with the same set of options, I shall come out with the same option as most appropriate for action. Thus, I concluded that the decision that a person with a definite personality makes in a particular situation is predetermined and so is the sequel to the extent it depends on it. With this a perception, which I had traditionally obtained, that thoughts come up in the brain at random was also destroyed.

E.3.2 *Realising the absolute predestinedness of the future*

I had great interest and aptitude in physics. I knew that the universe is made up of matter and energy, which follow the laws of nature in their transactions, yet the phenomena taking place in the universe were not considered going on in absolutely predestined way, mainly because most of the physicists thought that the principle of indeterminacy implies that there is inherent indefiniteness in whatever exists, and therefore it was a conviction in the scientific spheres that the future cannot be absolutely predestined.

The concept of indefiniteness had always been unacceptable to me.

I had realised that since the structure of the elementary constituents of the universe is not clear to us, the basic assumptions of quantum mechanics are probabilistic and that is why it is forced to talk in terms of probabilities. And since the principle of indeterminacy is an offspring of quantum mechanics, it too deals in probabilities: it relates the probabilities of finding the properties of things in definite ranges (see Appendix C, 'Physical significance of the principle of indeterminacy') and does in no way tell that the properties are indefinite themselves. Being unable to measure something accurately or being ignorant about something does not at all imply that that thing is indefinite or has indefinite properties, and therefore I never agreed with the school of thought that saw quantum mechanics or principle of indeterminacy as implying inherent indefiniteness in nature. In fact, from the very outset, I thought it was absurd and unscientific to think that anything can have indefinite characteristics. Thus, I was convinced that as far as the phenomena that involve only nonliving things are concerned, they occur in absolutely predestined way.

Though I knew that living things are also basically made up of nonliving material, I was not very confident that the phenomena associated with them follow a predestined course, because these phenomena are affected by the activities in their mental sphere, such as thoughts, plans, and dreams, about which I felt that they are ruled over by chaos to at least some extent. So I thought that if the universe were made up of only nonliving things, the future would be absolutely predestined. When I found that a complex phenomenon related to living things such as decision making goes on in a predestined way, no doubt was left in my mind and I became convinced that all the phenomena that take place in the universe, including thoughts, ideas, dreams, and so on, follow predetermined path and every bit of the future is absolutely predestined.

I reached this conclusion in 1993, when I was twenty-one years old. It eventually led me to the realisation of God.

E.3.3 *Finding God*

After I was logically and scientifically convinced that whatever happens is predestined; that nothing occurs at random; or that every phenomenon, event, or happening that takes place in the universe follows laws, it was self-evident to me that the whole universe is in absolute control of all the laws of nature put together, the set of all the laws of nature.

I had read books related to almost every major religion. I was aware that the concept of God is the hub of theistic religions and also that the hub of the concept of God or of whatever is believed about God is the belief that it is almighty, that is, one who exercises unconditional or absolute authority over the whole universe or one who governs the nature all by itself. Thus, after I realised that the set of all the laws of nature has complete authority over the universe, in a due course of time, it was natural for me to consider that it is God, although that its image did not exactly match with God's traditional image was making it difficult for me to believe in or to put into my heart my own consideration.

I thought that if none of the laws of nature is a part of God, it is something that does not have any authority, but since authority-less God is unimaginable or the belief that it is almighty, that it has absolute authority over the universe, lies at the core of the concept of God and since it is only the set of all the laws of nature that has absolute authority over the universe, I had no option but to accept it as a part of God or God itself, whether or not it exactly fits into the traditional image of God.

After I felt that God cannot be anything less than the set of all the laws of nature but can be larger than it, as time passed by, I thought on the possibility of other things that have it as their part or subset, such as the set that contains both the universe and the set of all the laws of nature and the set that contains all the strictly followed or infallible laws, including all the laws of nature and all the laws of mathematics, as God but could not see any of them matching the concept of God as closely as it is done by it, the set of all the laws of nature.

Thus, I concluded that the set of all the laws of nature is, and only is, God or God is nothing except the set of all the laws of nature. This happened when I was twenty-five years old, four years after I realised that the future is predestined and unchangeable.

E.4 CREDIT

It is true that I independently concluded that God is the set of all the laws of nature, without taking any thought or conclusion of anyone else as the starting point, but it is also true that I did not begin just from nothing. Whether it is the realisation of the absolute predestinedness of the future or the finding of God, both of them are based on the height of the progress in science and scientific attitude of our age. They have come up as a result of the demand of our time.

I have repeatedly said as well as shown in the book that whatever happens to or is done by a person is caused by the whole universe in the direction of God and is predestined. This stands true also for whatever happened to me and whatever deeds I performed, including realisation of the absolute predestinedness of the phenomena, events, or happenings that take place in the universe; the finding of God; and the creation of this book. Amen.

NOTES

NOTES TO CHAPTER 9: THE CONCEPT OF GOD

1. The correct way to write and pronounce the names of God 'Om Tat Sat' and 'Brahm' is 'Om Tut Sut' and 'Bruhm' respectively where 'u' sounds the same way as it does in 'but'.
2. The correct way to write and pronounce the name of Lord Rama is 'Ram' where 'a' sounds the same way as it does in 'far', 'par', or 'bar'.
3. The correct way to write and pronounce the name of Lord Krishna in English is 'Krishn'.
4. The correct way to write and pronounce the names of God 'Sat-Kartar' and 'Sat-Nam' is 'Sut-Kurtar' and 'Sut-Nam' respectively where 'u' sounds the same way as it does in 'but' and 'a' sounds the same way as it does in 'far'.
5. The correct way to write and pronounce the name of the creator god 'Brahma' is 'Bruhma' where 'u' sounds the same way as it does in 'but' and 'a' sounds the same way as it does in 'far'.
6. The correct way to write and pronounce the name of Lord Mahesh is 'Muhaish' where 'u' sounds the same way as it does in 'but' and 'ai' sounds the same way as it does in 'main' or as 'a' sounds in 'take'.

NOTES TO CHAPTER 13: WHY CAN ANY OTHER BEING NOT BE GOD?

1. See Chapter 9, note 2.
2. See Chapter 9, note 3.
3. The correct way to write and pronounce the name of Lord Buddha in English is 'Buddh' where 'u' sounds the same way as it does in 'put' or 'bull'.
4. Jebara, 'All things are numbers'.
5. Tipler, *The Physics of Immortality*.

NOTES TO CHAPTER 15: GOD AND RELIGION

1. See Chapter 9, note 1.
2. See Chapter 9, note 4.
3. See Chapter 13, note 3.
4. The correct way to write and pronounce 'samadhi' in English is 'sumadhi' where 'u' sounds the same way as it does in 'but' or 'sum' and 'i' sounds the same way as it does in 'in' or 'fish'.
5. The correct way to write and pronounce 'yoga' is 'yoag' where 'oa' sounds the same way as it does in 'road' or 'load'.

NOTES TO APPENDIX E: HOW DID I FIND GOD?

1. Weinberg, *Dreams of a Final Theory*, 195–96.
2. Hawking, 'Stephen Hawking Discusses Quantum Physics and ALS'.
3. Tipler, *The Physics of Immortality*.
4. The correct way to write and pronounce 'moksha' is 'moksh' where 'o' sounds the same way as it does in 'no' or 'gold'.
5. See Chapter 15, note 4.

BIBLIOGRAPHY

Aiken, Charles F. 'Confucianism'. Vol. 4 of *The Catholic Encyclopedia*. Robert Appleton Company, 1908. *Catholic Encyclopedia*. New Advent, 2004. http://www.newadvent.org/cathen/04223b.htm.

Beiser, Arthur. *Concepts of Modern Physics*. 5th ed. 4th reprint, New Delhi: Tata McGraw-Hill Publishing Company Limited, 1998.

Chan, Wing-Tsit, trans. *A Source Book in Chinese Philosophy*. Princeton: Princeton University Press, 1969.

Ebrey, Patricia Buckley, ed. *Chinese Civilization: A Sourcebook*. 2nd ed. New York: Free Press, 1993.

Encyclopedia Britannica Online, 2005. Encyclopedia Britannica Premium Service. *Encyclopedia Britannica*. 'Ahura Mazda'. http://www.britannica.com/eb/article-9004163.

———. 'Allah'. http://www.britannica.com/eb/article-9005770.

———. 'Biblical Literature'. http://www.britannica.com/eb/article-9110574.

———. 'Christianity'. http://www.britannica.com/eb/article-9105945.

———. 'Confucianism'. http://www.britannica.com/eb/article-9109629.

———. 'Confucius'. http://www.britannica.com/eb/article-9109630.

———. 'Islam'. http://www.britannica.com/eb/article-9105852.

———. 'Jen'. http://www.britannica.com/eb/article-9043513.

———. 'Jesus Christ'. http://www.britannica.com/eb/article-9106456.

———. 'Judaism'. http://www.britannica.com/eb/article-9105859.

———. 'Moses'. http://www.britannica.com/eb/article-9108742.

———. 'Taoism'. http://www.britannica.com/eb/article-9105866.

———. 'Tien'. http://www.britannica.com/eb/article-9072417.

———. 'Zoroaster'. http://www.britannica.com/eb/article-9078456.

———. 'Zoroastrianism'. http://www.britannica.com/eb/article-9106002.

Hawking, Stephen. 'Stephen Hawking Discusses Quantum Physics and ALS'. Interview by Larry King. *CNN Larry King Live*. CNN, 25 December 1999. Latest News – The Stephen Hawking Pages. Compiled by Nick Donaldson. *psyclops*, 1999. http://www.psyclops.com/hawking/resources/cnn.html.

Hooker, Richard. 'Tao'. China Glossary. *World Civilizations*. Washington State University. 14 July 1999. http://www.wsu.edu:8080/~dee/GLOSSARY/TAO.HTM.

———. 'Yin and Yang'. Chinese Philosophy. *World Civilizations*. Washington State University, 6 June 1999. http://www.wsu.edu:8080/~dee/CHPHIL/YINYANG.HTM.

Irani, Dinshah. 'Studying the Gathas as a Practical Guide to a Blissful Existence'. Foreword to *Metrical Version of The Gathas In English*, by Sorabjee Pestonjee Kanga. Mumbai, 1934. Reprint, Mumbai: Jenaz Printers, 1997. Gathic Illustration. *Vohuman.Org*. http://www.vohuman.org/Article/Studying%20the%20Gathas%20as%20a%20Pratical%20Guide%20to%20a%20Blissful%20Existence.htm.

Jebara, Adib Ben. 'All things are numbers'. Philosophy and the axiom. *Jebara*. FortuneCity.com, Inc., 2000. http://members.fortunecity.com/jebara/jebara/id2.html.

Khalsa, Sant Singh, trans. *Sri Guru Granth Sahib: English Translation*. CD-ROM. California: Orange County Sikh Centre, 2000. http://www.sikhs.org/english/frame.html.

Prasad, Ramanand, trans. *The Bhagavad Gita: The Song of God*. Originally, a part of the ancient Indian epic Mahabharat, by Ved Vyas. Fermont: International Gita Society, 1988. http://www.gita-society.com/section1/1_gitachapters.htm.

Rajam, J. B. *Atomic Physics*. 7th ed. 4th reprint, New Delhi: S. Chand & Co. (Pvt.) Ltd., 1974.

Rensselaer, Robert. 'Renovation Follows Renovation Without Cease'. *Sunrise: Theosophic Perspectives*, November 1976. *Sunrise: Theosophic Perspectives — bimonthly magazine*. Theosophical University Press Online Edition. Theosophical University Press. http://www.theosociety.org/pasadena/sunrise/26-76-7/rel-rens.htm.

Rodwell, J. M., trans. *The Koran*. With an introduction by G. Margoliouth. 12th ed. Illinois: Project Gutenberg, 2004. http://www.gutenberg.org/dirs/etext02/koran12a.txt.

Shreemadbhagwadgeetha [in Sanskrit and Hindi]. Originally, a part of the ancient Indian epic Mahabharat, by Ved Vyas. 23rd ed. Gorakhpur: Gita Press, 1975.

Tipler, Frank J. *The Physics of Immortality: Modern Cosmology, God and the Resurrection of the Dead*. New York: Anchor, 1997.

Weinberg, Steven. *Dreams of a Final Theory: The Search for the Fundamental Laws of Nature*. London: Vintage, 1993.

Worthing, Mark William. *God, Creation, and Contemporary Physics*. Minneapolis: Fortress Press, 1996.

ACKNOWLEDGEMENTS

The writing of *God and Destiny*, making its book proposal, and preparing its manuscript for review were solitary activities. But after that, through the process of its review and publication, I have received the help of many people.

Sabhajit Mishra and R A Singh reviewed the whole manuscript carefully for fundamental or theoretical errors related to the fields of philosophy and physics respectively. The questions posed and corrections suggested by them have helped in elevating the level of the book. The comments and suggestions of Sudhanshuji Maharaj, Hariharkripalu Tripathi, and Sagarika Ghose were priceless. I am grateful to all the reviewers for their time and effort.

I am very thankful to Arun Shourie, who is one of my heroes, for his invaluable help and guidance in the publication of the book. I am also obliged to Rajendra Awasthi, Jaswant Singh, Ashwani Chanan, Tushar Gandhi, Late L M Singhvi, Reema Huja, William Dalrymple, David Godwin, Indrajeet Hazra, Bharati Kirchener, and Anushka Ravishanker for their guidance in different aspects and stages of publishing of *God and Destiny*.

I am thankful to Rupa & Co. for providing a vast and credible platform for this book to be published and read. From acquisition of the manuscript to publication of the book, people from Rupa have worked enthusiastically on the project. Those whose role I am aware of are R K Mehra, Kapish Mehra, Vijay Kumaı Sharma, Sanjana Roy Choudhury, Trisha Bora, and Smita Singh. I am appreciative of team Rupa for their confidence in my work, for their contributions to the project, and for their patience with me. Thanks to Vivek Sahni Design for the appropriate cover design and to Raj John and Sanjay Gupta of Mindways Design for apt typesetting of the manuscript.

I have been working on *God and Destiny* full time since June 1998. Throughout this time my parents have supported me fully and have given me all possible help. Without their support, I am not sure whether I would have ever been able to accomplish this project. So this book is theirs as much as it is mine. Ma, pa, I do not have enough words or writing skill to thank you, to express my gratitude towards you.

Through all these years, my younger brother Vikas has remained my best friend. He has always recognised the value of my project and stood behind the cause. He has encouraged, helped, cheered, and criticised me whenever I needed. Whenever he provided any assistance to me (and that happened countless times), he amusingly demanded in return a percentage of my potential income from the book. I am indebted to you more than one hundred per cent bro.

I am thankful to Kalraj Mishra, Madhurji Maharaj, Bhupendra Chaubey, Sadakant Shukla, Dinesh Chandra Dubey, Maheshwar Mishra, Yagyeshwar Mishra, Prem Pathak, Rekha Pathak, Amit Shukla, Ragini Shukla, Umesh Mishra, Rekha Misra, Vijayanand Pandey, Rita Pandey, Chudamani Tripathi, Ganesh Datt Shukla, Paras Nath Shukla, Sudhir Kumar Shukla, Usha Shukla, Sunil Kumar Shukla, Anjana Shukla, Rajesh Mishra, Vijay Kumar Shukla, Anupama Shukla, Shitala Prasad Pandey, Ghanshyam Shukla, Anil Shukla, Indu Prakash Pathak, Neelam Pathak, Ravindra Kumar Shukla, Shailesh Kumar Mishra, and Ajit Kumar Srivastava for their respective help.

Finally, I express my gratitude towards Rajiv Mishra, Yasha Mishra, Mr & Mrs Jagat Pal Pathak, Pradeep Kumar Tripathi, Pushpa Tripathi, Noor Fatma, Sameer Kumar Shukla, Rashmi Shukla, Thakur Singh Mapwal, Tilak Singh Martolia, Manu Chopra, Rudresh Singh, Ashutosh Srivastava, Marjan Kheirollahi, Katihana Kirk, Faiz Ahmed, and N Ramachandra Rao for their love, care, encouragement, and support for me.

INDEX